T0248133

Advance Praise for *A Republic, If We Can Teach It*

"Lamentations about the sad state of civic education in today's American schools are as plentiful as the shells scattered on the summer seashore. But few of those critiques are able to provide us with a plausible way out of the mess we are in. Few are willing to ground civic education in a robust commitment to the American experiment in self-government; fewer still embrace the idea that the formation of responsible citizens is one of the most important jobs of our educational institutions. Sikkenga and Davenport, however, are welcome exceptions to these generalizations; and with the publication of this taut, lucid, courageous, and practical handbook for reform, they have staked out a path forward for us. May their voices be heard, and their efforts crowned with success."

—**Wilfred M. McClay**, Professor of History, Hillsdale College

"Sounding the alarm for an 'all hands on deck,' Davenport and Sikkenga make the compelling case that we need more and better civics education. Encouragingly, they provide practical solutions for everyone to do their part—families, communities, schools, and government. In short, they make it clear that our country has a crisis that must be addressed if we want to preserve our republic and prepare the next generation of informed patriots. If you want to do your part, this is a must-read."

—**Hanna Skandera**, President and CEO of the Daniels Fund, Former Secretary of Education of New Mexico

"In this principled yet practical guide to fixing civic education in America, Sikkenga and Davenport draw on their vast experience as well as careful scholarship. While pulling no punches about the seriousness of the present crisis, they avoid the hand-wringing and cultural warfare that afflict much of this field and shun pie-in-sky calls for a federal solution. Instead, their careful recommendations for state leaders and educators rightly center on standards, curriculum, and teacher prep, plus expanded civics (and history) instruction throughout the K–12 years, taught in ways that engage students and help them to become knowledgeable and discerning patriots."

—**Chester E. Finn, Jr.**, President Emeritus, Thomas B. Fordham Institute, and Volker Senior Fellow, Hoover Institution, Stanford University

A

REPUBLIC

—— If We Can ——

TEACH IT

A

REPUBLIC
—— *If We Can* ——
TEACH IT

Fixing America's Civic Education Crisis

JEFFREY SIKKENGA
& DAVID DAVENPORT

A REPUBLIC BOOK
ISBN: 978-1-64572-049-2
ISBN (eBook): 978-1-64572-050-8

A Republic, If We Can Teach It:
Fixing America's Civic Education Crisis
© 2024 by Jeffrey Sikkenga and David Davenport
All Rights Reserved

Cover Design by Jim Villaflores

Republic Book Publishers
New York, NY
www.republicbookpublishers.com

Published in the United States of America
1 2 3 4 5 6 7 8 9 10

TABLE OF CONTENTS

INTRODUCTION

In the hot summer of 1787, fifty-five delegates convened in Philadelphia and worked for months to draft a new constitution for the country. The story goes that as one of the Founders, Benjamin Franklin, exited Independence Hall at the end of the Convention, a local resident, Mrs. Powell, asked him what kind of government they had given us. Franklin famously responded, "A republic, if you can keep it." The Founders well understood that to live in a free republic requires both an educated and virtuous people. While the republic faces many threats today, none is more dangerous than the poor state of our civic education. We can only keep the republic if we can teach it!

In considering all of the problems America faces, we must remember to pay attention to our foundations. Perhaps you remember the shock when a twelve-story condo building in Miami, Florida, collapsed in the middle of the night on June 24, 2021. No one had imagined that such a tall ocean-front tower could essentially fall down, seemingly without warning, leaving human and family tragedy in its wake. Professionals continue to study the causes, but most believe it was a failure of structural and foundational support undergirding the building itself.

Sadly, this is a parable of a serious collapse threatening our body politic. For example, the Pew Research Center has studied Americans' trust in their government since 1958, and finds it is now "near historic lows" at only 24 percent. Even more troubling, trust in government among young people is lower still at 17 percent.[1] Only about 60 percent of Americans carry out perhaps their most important duty as citizens by voting, and even fewer (40 to 50 percent) in a midterm election. You might be surprised to learn that, based on 2020 data, the US places at a lowly thirty-two among thirty-seven highly developed democratic states in voter turnout.[2] Again, young people—who are not only the present but more importantly the future of our country—vote at even lower rates than the population as a whole.

The loss of trust and lack of participation are serious problems, but other cracks in our democracy have emerged as well. Hyperpartisan politics now dominate our government in Washington, DC, such that members of Congress find it difficult to agree to keep the government open or to pay its debts and avoid default. Important changes in policies are now enacted either by executive orders of the president or purely party-line votes in Congress, since bipartisanship is all but gone. The major political parties have gone to their separate corners and seem to care only about winning elections, not governing or finding the best policy solutions for America's problems.

---

[1] "Public Trust in Government: 1958-2023," Pew Research Center, September 19, 2023, https://www.pewresearch.org/politics/2021/05/17/public-trust-in-government-1958-2021/

[2] Drew DeSilver, "Turnout in U.S. has soared in recent elections but by some measures still trails that of many other countries," Pew Research Center, November 1, 2022, https://www.pewresearch.org/fact-tank/2020/11/03/in-past-elections-u-s-trailed-most-developed-countries-in-voter-turnout/

Following such patterns, too many young people are not even sure they believe in America and the American system any longer. In recent years, surveys show that Americans in their late teens and twenties are increasingly open to socialism, and even communism—ideas long considered antithetical to the American system.

The Infrastructure Has Decayed

We have come to recognize that America's basic infrastructure—its roads, bridges, airports and the like—are decaying and in need of repair. Although politicians in Washington, DC, may disagree on the amount of spending needed for this, there is a growing consensus that a major investment must be made to strengthen and renew our public infrastructure.

That is precisely where we are with the infrastructure of our democracy. We have allowed the very foundation of our republic—Americans' understanding of our history, our principles, and our duties as citizens—to decay all around us. Federal spending for civic education has dropped dramatically, and we have allowed it to be pushed to the edge of the curriculum by state standards and school decisions. Consequently, the very civic foundations of our country have been allowed to decay, and we are now reaping the harvest of generations not educated or committed to the American way. Indeed, most of the major problems in our democracy that we describe, if not caused by poor civic education, would at least be improved, and perhaps even solved, by better civic education.

This was the plan from the beginning: Americans would develop a strong understanding of civics and would be engaged in the ongoing work of democracy. As Notre Dame scholar David Campbell has said, "[C]ivics is not superfluous or even secondary to the primary purpose of public schooling. It is the primary purpose." He goes on to point out that "US public schools were actually created for the express purpose of forming democratic citizens."[3] The Founders understood that living in a free society required an informed and virtuous people which, in turn, depended on robust civic education. As Thomas Jefferson wrote, "The qualifications for self-government in society are not innate. They are the result of habit and long training."[4] In this regard, we are truly failing the future generations of citizens.

The evidence of this growing civics crisis surrounds us. Perhaps the most obvious data points are the results of the National Assessment of Educational Progress (NAEP) testing, often called "the nation's report card." This standardized national test is administered regularly in certain subjects such as reading and math at multiple grade levels. Unfortunately, US history and civics are now tested only among eighth graders. The latest test results show a disappointing 24 percent of American eighth graders are "proficient" or "better" in civics and government, and a shocking 15 percent are "proficient" in US history. The 2020 report shows statistically significant declines for male, female, white, black and Hispanic students—in other words, across the board. Then US secretary of education Betsy DeVos rightly called these scores "stark and inexcusable." A further

---

[3] David E. Campbell, "Introduction," in Making Civics Count: Citizenship Education for a New Generation, ed. David E. Campbell, Meira Levinson, and Frederick M. Hess (Massachusetts: Harvard Education Press, 2012), 2.

[4] Thomas Jefferson to Edward Everett, March 27, 1824, https://tjrs.monticello.org/letter/1661.

testing data point confirms this poor performance. Of forty-five Advanced Placement tests administered in 2019, scores in both government and US history were among the five lowest subjects tested.[5]

Other surveys and studies show the widening effect of this profound lack of knowledge of our history and principles as well as understanding of our civic duties. A study by the Institute for Citizens & Scholars found that only one in three Americans could pass the American citizenship test,[6] which immigrants pass at more than a 90 percent rate. The Annenberg Public Policy Center has been publishing an annual report on civic knowledge since 2006. Its 2019 report showed that 37 percent of Americans could not name a single right guaranteed by the First Amendment to the Constitution. Beyond that, too many people do not know the three branches of government. Indeed, some students have said they think Judge Judy is on the Supreme Court and that climate change was started by the Cold War.

Unfortunately, things are not only bad but seem to be moving in the wrong direction. Civic knowledge is consistently worse among younger Americans than older generations, suggesting that current civic education programs are truly failing. A 2018 Pew Research Center study showed that whereas 19 percent of those over sixty-five had "low" civic knowledge, that figure jumped to 41 percent among those aged eighteen

[5] Halle Edwards, "These Are the Hardest AP Classes and Tests For You," PrepScholar, November 13, 2022, https://blog.prepscholar.com/hardest-ap-classes-and-tests

[6] "National Survey Finds Just 1 in 3 Americans Would Pass Citizenship Test," Institute for Citizens & Scholars, October 3, 2018, https://citizensandscholars.org/resource/national-survey-finds-just-1-in-3-americans-would-pass-citizenship-test/.

to twenty-nine.[7] When the Institute for Citizens & Scholars reported on Americans who could pass the immigration test, they found that 74 percent of those over sixty-five could answer six of ten questions correctly, but only 19 percent of those under forty-five could do so. A significant reduction in school course requirements in civic education over the last fifty years would easily account for these differences.

All these declining numbers should sound an alarm that our civic infrastructure is badly decayed. We are raising a generation of leaders and citizens who lack the basic knowledge needed to understand, much less lead, our republic. Just as we would not turn over our health to doctors who lacked knowledge of basic anatomy or how the human body operates, we should be equally frightened about turning over our government to citizens and leaders who do not understand how and why the political and economic systems function as they do. No need to wait for the building to collapse in the middle of the night—we must act now.

The Downstream Effects of Our Civic Education Crisis

Beyond the lack of civic knowledge and understanding, we can see the effects of the civic education crisis rippling out through our society. In several arenas, there are major societal and political problems whose roots can be traced to poor civic education. In fact, as political polarization, election challenges, and other problems with our democratic processes grow, larger numbers

---

[7] "Demographic Differences in Levels of Civic Knowledge," Pew Research Center, April 26, 2018, https://www.pewresearch.org/politics/2018/04/26/10-political-engagement-knowledge-and-the-midterms/

of people are beginning to wonder whether more civic education is needed. Some have even wondered whether the lack of robust civic education creates a national security problem for the United States.

It does seem clear that several aspects of American democracy would function better if there was more and better civic education. The most obvious of these would be greater faith in our constitutional institutions, a higher voter turnout, and better understanding of the tough policy issues America faces.

The loss of faith in institutions, especially among young people, has become an alarming problem. How can you trust what you do not understand? The Pew Research Center issued a "wide-ranging" survey on questions of trust in 2019, showing that young people, especially, have low levels of trust for a wide range of institutions—including government—and their leaders.[8] Only 33 percent of young people expressed trust in business executives, 27 percent in elected leaders, and 47 percent in journalists. Only two categories of leaders—science and the military—were trusted. In most cases, the difference in trust levels among younger people were 15 to 20 percent lower than in older Americans. A similar study, the Edelman Trust Barometer, found that none of four social institutions studied—government, business, NGOs, and the media—is trusted.[9]

---

[8] John Gramlich, "Young Americans are less trusting of other people – and key institutions – than their elders," Pew Research Center, August 6, 2019, https://www.pewresearch.org/fact-tank/2019/08/06/young-americans-are-less-trusting-of-other-people-and-key-institutions-than-their-elders/.

[9] "2021 Edelman Trust Barometer," Edelman, January 13, 2021, https://www.edelman.com/sites/g/files/aatuss191/files/2021-03/2021%20Edelman%20Trust%20Barometer.pdf

Yuval Levin, in his important book *A Time to Build*, advances its argument from this straightforward premise: "Everybody knows that Americans having long been losing faith in institutions."[10] But the loss of trust in government and its leaders is especially serious. Of the several leaders and occupations identified in the Pew Research Center study, elected officials are trusted the least—only 27 percent—by young people. By comparison, older Americans expressed trust at a 46 percent rate. One might say that the opposite of trust is alienation—another topic studied by Pew since 1958, finding that only 24 percent of Americans trust government to "do what is right" most of the time.[11] Trust in all three branches of the federal government has plummeted.

The problem with lack of trust is not, of course, that people will fail to rely on government programs to solve social or economic problems. Rather, they will not accept the legitimacy of our constitutional institutions, which are the way we carry out our experiment in self-government. As one study pointed out: "Those who are bewildered by such basics as the branches of government and the concept of judicial review are less likely to trust the courts.... Importantly, those who have taken a high school civics class are more likely to command key constitutional concepts."[12] The cost of this lack of knowledge is high: if we lose

---

[10] Yuval Levin, A Time To Build (New York: Basic Books, 2020), 3.
[11] "Public Trust in Government: 1958-2023," Pew Research Center, September 19, 2023, https://www.pewresearch.org/politics/2021/05/17/public-trust-in-government-1958-2021/.
[12] "Guardian of Democracy: The Civic Mission of Schools," ed. Jonathan Gould, 2003, 4–5, http://cdn.annenbergpublicpolicycenter.org/wp-content/uploads/GuardianofDemocracy_report_final-12.pdf.

trust in the institutions of constitutional self-government, we lose faith in our ability to govern ourselves.

There needs to be more research documenting what seems like an inevitable link between poor civic education and a lack of trust in the institutions of constitutional self-government, but it makes good sense. Even at a psychological level, we understand that ignorance easily produces fear and frustration whereas knowledge can form a basis for trust. A study by the Civic Mission of Schools concluded that mistrust of institutions "would be ameliorated by a more knowledgeable and engaged citizenry."[13] Even if civic education is not the cause of mistrust, it could be the solution. As Katherine Barrett and Richard Greene wrote, "How, indeed, can anyone trust a powerful entity they don't understand. It's a basic element of human nature that ignorance leads inevitably to mistrust."[14]

Poor civic education and low trust lead to a further problem: low voter turnout and lack of civic participation by young people. Voting is a fundamental right, perhaps *the* fundamental right and responsibility in a democracy. It is the people's opportunity to be heard and the means by which a representative government of, by, and for the people is chosen. As Thomas Paine said in his *Dissertation on First Principles of Government*, "The right of voting for representatives is the primary right by which other rights are protected."

---

[13] Ibid., 5.

[14] Katherine Barrett and Richard Greene, "Civic Education: A Key to Trust in Government," American Political Science Association, October 17, 2017, https://politicalsciencenow.com/civic-education-a-key-to-trust-in-government/.

One important measure of the health of a republic is the level of citizen participation in voting. It is of real concern, then, that US voting rates are low, especially among younger voters. As one report summarized it, "The voter turnout rate in US presidential elections has fallen from a high of 69.3 percent in 1964 to a low of 54.7 percent in 2000, hovering now around 60 percent."[15] The voting rates in midterm elections are even lower, at 40–50 percent. In data published by the Organization for Economic Cooperation and Development earlier than 2020, US voting rates are surprisingly low compared to other highly developed democratic states, placing twenty-sixth out of thirty-two nations.[16] When barely half the people are turning out to vote, one worries about the health of a self-governing republic and the disengagement of the citizenry.

While low voter turnout is a significant concern, it is especially troubling that young people continue to turn out at a significantly lower rate than other age groups. Alia Wong pointed out in *The Atlantic* that only half of eligible adults eighteen to twenty-nine voted in the 2016 presidential election and only 20 percent in the 2014 midterm election.[17] When comparing generations, whereas only half of younger voters turned out in

---

[15] Zhaogang Quiao et al., "Does More Education Promote Civic Engagement?" Journal of Postdoctoral Research, vol. 5, no. 9 (2017), 33–34.

[16] Drew DeSilver, "Turnout in U.S. has soared in recent elections but by some measures still trails that of many other countries," Pew Research Center, November 1, 2022, https://www.pewresearch.org/short-reads/2022/11/01/turnout-in-u-s-has-soared-in-recent-elections-but-by-some-measures-still-trails-that-of-many-other-countries/.

[17] Alia Wong, "Civics Education Helps Create Young Voters And Activists," The Atlantic, October 5, 2018, https://www.theatlantic.com/education/archive/2018/10/civics-education-helps-form-young-voters-and-activists/572299/.

2016, two-thirds of the older age groups voted.[18] Voter turnout was higher across the board in 2020, though with the longer-term trend of low voting rates, one wonders whether that was more likely an aberration rather than a new trend.[19]

Experts agree that there is a correlation between improved civic education and increased voting rates. (Actually, evidence shows that education itself—not just civic education—is a predictor of higher levels of voting.[20]) Civic education in particular results in increased civic participation, including voting. A study by scholar Jennifer Bachner concluded, "Students who complete a year of American Government or Civics are 3-6 percentage points more likely to vote than their peers without such a course and 7-11 percentage points more likely to vote than peers who do not discuss politics at home."[21] This report concluded, "The only course that consistently exerts a positive effect on voting behavior is American Government/Civics."[22] Testing students'

---

[18] Thom File, "Voting in America: A Look at the 2016 Presidential Election," United States Census Bureau, May 10, 2017, https://www.census.gov/newsroom/blogs/random-samplings/2017/05/voting_in_america.html

[19] See, e.g., "Half of Youth Voted in 2020, An 11-Point Increase from 2016," Center for Information & Research on Civic Learning and Engagement, April 29, 2021, https://circle.tufts.edu/latest-research/half-youth-voted-2020-11-point-increase-2016.

[20] Quiao et al., "Does More Education," 33–38.

[21] Jennifer Bachner, "From Classroom to the Voting Booth: The Effect of High School Civic Education on Turnout," Scribd, September 12, 2010, https://www.scribd.com/document/122825938/From-Classroom-to-Voting-Booth-The-Eff-ect-of-High-School-Civic-Education-on-Turnout-Jennifer-Bachner.

[22] Ibid, 19.

civic knowledge has also been shown to improve turnout among young voters.[23]

In fact, an interesting civic education experiment would be to allow sixteen- and seventeen-year-olds to pre-register as voters in class before they turn eighteen and become legally able to vote. This idea has gained some momentum with a number of states implementing it.[24] Including pre-registration as part of the civics curriculum would boost voter turnout among the young and is surely a better solution than proposals to allow sixteen- and seventeen-year-olds to vote.[25]

Not only does poor civic education contribute to a lack of trust in our systems and leaders and lead to low voter turnout, but it also distorts important policy debates and decisions. If whole generations have not been well-educated about the American system and how and why it works as it does, it should not be surprising that our conversations about America are thrown off-track by this lack of knowledge and understanding.

A classic example of poor civic education distorting policy preferences is the recent increase in support among young people for socialism in America. Previously thought of as anathema to most Americans, socialism has now become popular, even

---

[23] Jason Giersch & Christopher Dong, "Required Civics Courses, Civics Exams and Voter Turnout," The Social Science Journal 55:2 (2018), 160–167.

[24] Sarah D. Sparks, "How States and Schools Are Working to Grow Young Voters," Education Week, March 6, 2020, https://www.edweek.org/teaching-learning/how-states-and-schools-are-working-to-grow-young-voters/2020/03.

[25] David Davenport, "Don't let 16-year-olds rock the vote," Washington Examiner, May 3, 2018, https://www.washingtonexaminer.com/opinion/dont-let-16-year-olds-rock-the-vote.

trendy, among younger generations. A number of polls and surveys in recent years attest to this rising acceptance of socialism.

As early as 2014, a Reason-Rupe study showed that 58 percent of young people aged eighteen to twenty-four held a favorable view of socialism.[26] This interest continued to manifest itself during the 2020 election cycle. A September 2020 YouGov poll showed 49 percent support for socialism among Gen Zers (ages sixteen to twenty-three).[27] Nearly half of American young people have even expressed a preference for living in a socialist country,[28] and one poll showed 36 percent of Gen Zers and millennials had a favorable view of communism.[29] Clearly something profoundly troubling has taken hold among young Americans.

While the favorability of socialism is heavily generational, it is also educational. Whereas the classic definition of socialism is "an economic system in which the people, usually through the government, own the means of production and distribution," this is apparently not what young people are supporting. Gallup published a poll on the meaning of socialism in October 2018 and found the following top three understandings of the term: equality (23 percent of respondents), government ownership and control of business (21 percent), and free services from the

---

[26] Emily Ekins, "Poll: Americans Like Free Markets More than Capitalism and Socialism More Than a Govt Managed Economy," Reason Magazine, February 12, 2015, https://reason.com/2015/02/12/poll-americans-like-free-markets-more-th/.

[27] "2020 Poll," Victims of Communism Memorial Foundation, https://victimsofcommunism.org/annual-poll/2020-annual-poll/.

[28] Kight, "Exclusive poll."

[29] "2019 Poll."

government (10 percent).[30] For every respondent who understood the classic definition of "government control of business,"
two thought socialism meant equality and free goods. Not far
down the list of definitions, at 6 percent, came "talking to people, being social…." In a 2010 *New York Times*/CBS poll, only
16 percent of young people could accurately define socialism.

Digging a little deeper, one finds a direct contradiction
between young people's favorable view of socialism and their
preference for who should run business. In the 2014 Reason-
Rupe survey, 58 percent of young people held a favorable view
of socialism. Later in that same survey, however, when asked
whether they wanted government or businesses leading the economy, they preferred markets by a two-to-one margin. Likewise,
the May 2019 Gallup poll found that 43 percent said socialism
would be good for the country with respondents then saying
they would choose market control over government control of
everything from the economy to wealth distribution and even
healthcare. Clearly, people are saying "socialism" when they do
not understand or intend the classic understanding of the term.

Identifying Denmark and other Scandinavian countries as
examples of desirable socialist economies provides further evidence of how the lack of education has created an increased
interest in socialism. Senator Bernie Sanders and others have
used Denmark as an example of the kind of socialist, or democratic socialist, economy that is desirable but—when you look
more closely—Denmark is not socialist either. With all the attention brought on his country during the 2016 US presidential

---

[30] Frank Newport, "The Meaning of 'Socialism' in America Today, Gallup, October 4, 2018, https://news.gallup.com/opinion/polling-mat-
ters/243362/meaning-socialism-americans-today.aspx.

election, then Danish prime minister Lars Lokke Rasmussen felt the need to clarify that Denmark was not socialist but rather "a market economy" with "an expanded welfare state."

It turns out that when young people say they like socialism, what they really like is an expanded welfare state and more free stuff, but their inability to understand and articulate correctly what socialism is has led to a lot of debate and discomfort about young Americans becoming socialist. These are matters that should be addressed and corrected by a solid civic education. Indeed, better civic education could address many problems in our democracy, from the lack of trust to poor voter turnout and civic participation to misguided contentions and debates about the American system. Perhaps poor civic education is not a root cause of many of these problems, but in any event, better civic education would be part of the solution.

A Slow Awakening

It is surprising that there is not a major campaign to improve civic education nationwide. With all this evidence and the resulting downstream problems, you would think there would be shouting from the rooftops, coupled with a robust campaign to strengthen civic education. But, alas, this is not the case. There is at least, however, a kind of slow awakening to the problem. Teachers now believe the emphasis on civics should be greater, with a 2019 poll showing 81 percent of teachers (and 70 percent of Americans) feeling the subject should be required.[31]

---

[31] "Frustration in the Schools," Phi Delta Kappan, vol. 101, no. 1 (2019), https://kappanonline.org/magazine-issue/frustration-in-the-schools/.

Now we have reached a crossroads. Too many young people, and even older Americans, know too little about their country, its history, and its government. While frustration and disgust with politics has led some to renew their civic engagement, especially by engaging at the local level with institutions like school boards, it also has led many to give up on civic engagement of any kind. STEM and other subjects have taken center stage in the school curriculum and have pushed civic education to the edges. Teachers are poorly trained and ill-equipped to teach civics. If we do not take a stand now to reemphasize civic education, the decline in both civic knowledge and engagement is likely to accelerate and cross a point from which it would be difficult, if not impossible, to return.

A Major Push for More and Better Civic Education

What we need is "all hands on deck" for more and better civic education. By "*more*" we mean teaching history and civics again in elementary and middle school instead of waiting until high school when it is truly too little, too late. By "*more*" we mean a required high school course of one year, not just one semester, in every state in the nation.

More civic education also requires more testing. The Nation's Report Card test, now given only to eighth graders in civics and US history, needs to be administered in the fourth and twelfth grades as well, with results reported by state for analysis and planned improvements. More testing could also include a civics test at the end of the one-year course as a graduation requirement, as a number of states have done.

More civic education also means more teacher training: they need greater content knowledge themselves in US history and civics, which will be even more essential if new coursework is required throughout the grade levels. Teaching civics must be more than a part-time duty that teachers pick up to round out their teaching load. State requirements for teachers need to be tougher and more specific.

As well as *more* civic education, we also need *better* civic education—far more than rote memorization of dates and facts. Students need to be engaged in the study of history and civics, not just exposed to them. We need to start in elementary school to build a "layer cake" of knowledge, adding more each year as the students' age and maturity allow. We need to engage students not only in the *what* of American history and government, but the *how* and the *why*. Students need to be inspired by the stories of their history and challenged by its debates and tough issues. They need to be exposed to primary documents of the day that illuminate the issues and arguments of civics and history, not just reading boring and often biased textbooks. They need teachers who know and are excited about the material.

Meanwhile, civics needs to be everyone's responsibility, not just that of school teachers. We need parents talking about America at the dinner table, taking their children to historic sites, challenging them to read great histories and biographies, and discussing current events and the news of the day. We need community groups distributing primary documents and sponsoring debates, speech contests, and civics bees.

Only when we can bring "all hands on deck" for civic education will we begin to turn around this national decline in civic knowledge and engagement. As President Reagan pointed out, the responsibility begins with families: parents sharing their sense of patriotism and civic engagement and passing these priorities along to their children. Next, the torch passes to the schools who need to carry out their civic education responsibilities beginning not in high school, but in kindergarten.

States may be the most important players of all in that they make curricular decisions by which their schools must abide. It is at the state level—legislatures and school boards—where requirements to teach civics are established. If we are to have civics taught at every grade, it must be mandated at the state level. If we seek to require a full-year high school course in civics, the states will need to require it. If there is to be a graduation test in civics, that duty falls to states. State school boards are also where teacher training and accreditation for teaching civics and US history should be established. We need states studying best practices in the teaching of history and civics and demanding that they be followed. A recent study by the Fordham Institute indicate that most states have a long way to go in this regard.[32]

Even Washington, DC, has a role to play. Perhaps the most valuable thing our national leaders can do is to speak out about the need to improve civic education. If, as seems likely, Washington will continue to spend money on K–12 education, civics needs to be at the table. Ideally, Washington would provide funding but not attempt to dictate to states how civics should be taught. Perhaps the best use of federal funding would be for content education for teachers, as was done in an earlier time.

---

[32] Jeremy A. Stern et al., "The State of State Standards for Civics and U.S. History in 2021," Thomas B. Fordham Institute, June 23, 2021, https://fordhaminstitute.org/national/research/state-state-standards-civics-and-us-history-2021.

Finally, the nonprofit sector can make a major contribution to the improvement of civic education. For example, our organization, the Ashbrook Center, has grown dramatically in its outreach to history and government teachers and their students. A new civics bee sponsored by the US Chamber of Commerce Foundation is another great idea. Other civic groups pass out founding documents at schools and provide educational materials. All this plays a vital role in strengthening civic education.

Essentially, everyone can and should play a role. As Chief Justice John Roberts said, "We have let civics fall by the wayside and we need to revive it in order to protect our democracy. We cannot afford to wait any longer to meet this challenge."

CHAPTER ONE

Our Sputnik Moment

We know from experience that when we neglect something, it usually deteriorates. When we neglect diet and exercise, we get flabby and become more subject to disease. When we neglect to charge our cellphone or computer, the battery dies. When we fail to keep up with our finances, we sink into debt. It is a principle we see in effect every day: when we ignore problems, they do not go away; they get worse.

This is the story of civic education in our time. It is not so much that educators made a conscious decision not to emphasize it or that our society or government made a deliberate decision to neglect civic education or replace it as a priority in the education of America's young people. Rather, we began to neglect civic education at all levels until it has fallen into disrepair. Further, new emphases in K–12 education crowded their way into the curriculum, making it difficult for civics to hold its ground.

As recently as the 1960s, there was a much greater emphasis on civic education in schools, with multiple courses taught at least at the high school level. However, the 1960s also saw America's response to the Soviet launch of Sputnik in 1957. When the Soviet Union became the first into outer space, America awakened to a need for both a more aggressive space program and improved and expanded science and math curriculum in our schools. Without expanding the school day or school year, curriculum can only increase in one area by reductions elsewhere, with both civics and US history losing ground.

Similar "crises" affected the K–12 curriculum in the decades to follow, nearly always at the expense of civic education. The *A Nation at Risk* report in 1983 underscored falling test scores among US students, especially compared with those of other industrialized countries, and led to educational reforms. The No Child Left Behind Law in 2002 introduced time-consuming testing in reading and math throughout the schools, especially in the elementary years, again at the expense of teaching time for social studies and the humanities. Then in the 1990s and today, STEM became all the rage in an effort to keep Americans competitively positioned for jobs in the new information economy. Many of these new educational emphases call for skill development in more than the teaching of knowledge, which has further hampered the teaching of civics. None of these initiatives directly targeted losses to civic education, but that was the unintended consequence.

From there, the neglect of civic education began to spread. Class time and course requirements for civic education declined. Spending on civics, especially at the federal level, nearly disappeared. Very little testing of civics was done, especially in comparison to reading and math, which delivered a strong message about priorities (especially in the kind of testing environment now created in the schools). By almost any measure, America had come to neglect civic education. By now, student learning in the field is so dismal that we have reached a crossroads from which it will be difficult to turn back.

States Neglect Civic Education

As a case study in how little states might do in civic education, a trip to Rhode Island is in order. Though the smallest of the states in territory (forty-eight miles long by thirty-seven miles wide), it was one of the thirteen original colonies and was founded by Roger Williams, a prominent religious dissenter who cared deeply about a healthy civic life. One would think history and civics would be robust in "Little Rhody," but that turns out not to be the case.

Until recently, Rhode Island was one of several states that did not require passing a single high school course in civics. Like many states, it also did not require the teaching of civics throughout elementary and middle school, which would ideally build toward a required high school course. In short, Rhode Island simply had not answered the civic education bell.

This neglect of civic education was uncovered in a shocking way a few years ago when fourteen Rhode Island high school students sued the governor and various education officials in federal court for violating their constitutional right to a civic education. The students argued that their failure to receive an adequate civic education left them without the skills or knowledge to carry out basic civic responsibilities, such as voting or serving on a jury. The lawsuit left the state of Rhode Island in the awkward position of arguing that, as their attorney

Anthony Cottone put it, "There is no fundamental right to education under the Constitution."[33]

In the end, the federal judge decided that the students had no constitutional right to civic education, while nevertheless castigating Rhode Island for failing to provide it.[34] US district court judge William Smith characterized the lawsuit as "a cry for help from a generation of young people who are destined to inherit a country which we—the generation currently in charge—are not stewarding well." Judge Smith went on to say that the student plaintiffs "seem to recognize that American democracy is in peril" and that "we would do well to pay attention to their plea." Even though he could not uphold their constitutional claim, Smith said the case nevertheless highlighted "a deep flaw in our national education priorities and policies" and he wished to add the court's "voice to plaintiffs' in calling attention to their plea."[35]

The court case was remarkable in several ways. First, the fact that students brought it at all, showing more appreciation than their public officials for the need of better civic education. Second, the judge, who could not constitutionally offer relief, nevertheless sided with the students on the woeful lack of civic education in the state. Lastly, perhaps

[33] Stacy Teicher Khadaroo, "Rhode Island lawsuit: Students sue for the right to learn civics," The Christian Science Monitor, December 12, 2019, https://www.csmonitor.com/USA/Education/2019/1212/Rhode-Island-lawsuit-Students-sue-for-the-right-to-learn-civics.

[34] A.C. v. Raimondo, 494 F. Supp. 3d 170 (D.R.I. 2020).

[35] The United States Court of Appeals for the First Circuit later affirmed the lower court decision, holding that there was no constitutional, fundamental right to civic education. A.C. v. Raimondo, 494 F. Supp. 3d 170 (D.R.I. 2020).

most important, it appears that while students lost the battle, they may nevertheless win the war. Not long after, the Rhode Island Senate passed a bill requiring civics education to be taught in schools.[36] As the bill's sponsor rightly said, "Solid civics education in public schools is absolutely critical to having an informed public." The bill has recently been signed by the governor, and Rhode Island will belatedly begin requiring civic education with the class of 2023.[37] The students have reached an agreement with the state's Commissioner of Education that they will not pursue further appeals and she in turn will establish a civic education task force.[38]

If we want more civic education in the schools, the states are the place to start. Education policy belongs primarily to the states and local governments—through property tax funding and school boards. Although several federal initiatives of the last twenty years—George W. Bush's No Child Left Behind Act, Barack Obama's Race to the Top, the Common Core curriculum—threatened to centralize more of education policy in Washington, DC, these federalizing efforts were substantially dialed back by the Every Student Succeeds Act (ESSA) in 2015.

[36] RI Gen L § 16-22-2 (2012).

[37] Rory Schuler, "Rhode Island Governor signs legislation requiring Civics Education in schools," Johnston Sun Rise, September 24, 2021, https://johnstonsunrise.net/stories/rhode-island-governor-signs-legislation-requiring-civics-education-in-schools,167501.

[38] Patricia Lamiell, "Rhode Island Lawsuit, Filed by the Center for Educational Equity at TC, Ends with Agreement to Improve Civic Education," Teachers College Columbia University, June 10, 2022, https://www.tc.columbia.edu/articles/2022/june/rhode-island-lawsuit-ends-with-agreement-to-improve-civics-education/.

The message of ESSA was that states are still in the driver's seat of K–12 education policy and decision-making.

The key civic education decisions for states are whether and how much history and civics to require in schools and whether there should be a statewide civics test (perhaps as a high school graduation requirement). The amount of time committed to teaching and learning US history and civics is doubtless the single most important variable in strengthening American civic education. Yet, some states require no civic education and the majority do not require enough. Statewide civics requirements, then, are a public policy question that should be taken up by governors, state legislatures, and boards of education.

A 2018 report by *Education Week* found that forty states require a course in US history with fifteen states also requiring a test to graduate.[39] Twenty-eight of the forty states require a year-long course.[40] The same study reported that only thirty-six states require a course in civics and government, with nineteen requiring a test to graduate and only eight requiring a year-long course. Only twenty-five states require even a one-semester course in high school on American history before the Civil War, and for most students, eighth grade is the last time they will study the

[39] Forty states requiring civics was also reported by the Center for American Democracy in 2019. Ashley Jeffrey and Scott Sargrad, "Strengthening Democracy With a Modern Civics Education," Center for American Progress, December 14, 2019, https://www.americanprogress.org/issues/education-k-12/reports/2019/12/14/478750/strengthening-democracy-modern-civics-education/.

[40] Debra Viadero et al., "Data: Most States Require History, But Not Civics," Education Week, October 23, 2018, https://www.edweek.org/teaching-learning/data-most-states-require-history-but-not-civics.

American founding.[41] With constant changes in requirements and even some differences in reporting, other studies have found similar, though not always identical, results. In its March 2020 report *Inspired to Serve*, the National Commission on Military, National and Public Service concluded that forty-four states, plus the District of Columbia, require civics or government as a condition of high school graduation.

Not only is the US several states short of the very basic goal of all students being required to take American history and civics courses, but most states only mandate a single one-semester course on American government rather than a full year of civics. According to the 2018 *Education Week* report, only eight states require a full year of civics and government (although Hawaii requires more than that). *Education Week* indicates that nineteen states require a civics test to graduate. If, as we will present in Chapter Six, a full-year course and a test represent the gold standard for high school civics, the majority of states have a long way to go to strike civic education gold.

In Schools, Civic Education Has Lost Out to Other Curricular Demands

With so little civic education required by state standards, and under heavy competition for curricular requirements demanded by testing regimes in math and reading as well as STEM education, it is not surprising that schools are not doing nearly enough to teach civics and government. In fact, it would be largely correct to say that civics and history—along with other courses in social

---

[41] TK.

science and the humanities—have been pushed out of school curricula by the newer emphasis on STEM and the regime of constant testing in reading and math imposed by the No Child Left
Behind law. There are only so many hours in the school day and
only a certain number of days in the school year, so if you increase
teaching of one thing, that time has to be taken from something
else. The loser in the curricular battle has been civic education.

Following the enactment of No Child Left Behind in 2002,
schools moved to increase their teaching of reading and math.
One 2007 study by the Center on Education Policy found
that 62 percent of school districts increased their study time
of English language arts (ELA) and math by an astonishing 43
percent.[42] At the same time, to accommodate this increase, 44
percent of districts reported cutting time for social studies and
other subjects by an average of 32 percent, with some schools
cutting teaching time in these areas by more than 50 percent.[43]

Reductions in teaching time for social studies, including civics, were especially pronounced in the elementary grades, where
they were already a low priority. Teachers in those grades now
spend as little as five percent of instruction time on history and
social studies.[44] As developmental psychologist William Damon

---

[42] Jennifer McMurrer, "Choices, Changes, and Challenges: Curriculum and
Instruction in the NCLB Era," Center on Education Policy (December
2007), a report in the series From the Capitol to the Classroom: Year 5
of the No Child Left Behind Act 8–9, http://www.schoolinfosystem.org/
pdf/2008/artsed.pdf.

[43] Ibid.

[44] Paul G. Fitchett et al., "An Analysis of Time Prioritization for Social Studies in Elementary School Classrooms, Journal of Curriculum and Instruction, vol. 8 (2014), 7–9. See also: Natalie Wexler, The Knowledge Gap:
The Hidden Cause of America's Broken Education System—And How to
Fix It (New York: Avery, 2019), 42.

has written, "Civics is one of the 'peripheral' subjects deemphasized by the single-minded focus on basic skills during the recent heyday of the narrow curriculum."[45]

Further blows to the civics curriculum were sustained when STEM education became emphasized. STEM seeks to steer schools toward a more technical, career-based education to enable Americans to better compete in the new information age. The STEM commitment has been huge, with federal spending to total some $3 billion per year. Even though relatively few students will turn out to major or work in these fields, STEM nevertheless seeks to add ten thousand new qualified STEM teachers to the education workforce and to increase the number of students having a STEM experience by 50 percent.[46]

The net result of these new priorities is a significant reduction in the teaching of civics compared to earlier times. Typically all that is required these days is a single one-semester course in high school. As one study noted, this "contrasts with course requirements in the 1960s, when three required courses in civics and government were common and civics was woven through the K–12 curriculum."[47] The same study adds, "Today, almost

[45] William Damon, "Restoring Purpose and Patriotism to American Education," in Michael J. Petrilli and Chester E. Finn, Jr., How to Educate an American: The Conservative Vision for Tomorrow's Schools (West Conshohocken, PA: Templeton Press, 2020), 81.

[46] Boris Granovskiy, Science, Technology, Engineering, and Mathematics (STEM) Education, Congressional Research Service, June 12, 2019, https://files.eric.ed.gov/fulltext/ED593605.pdf.

[47] Jan Brennan, "ESSA: Mapping Opportunities for Civic Education," Education Commission of the States, April, 2017, 5. https://files.eric.ed.gov/fulltext/ED574090.pdf.

two-thirds of teachers report that they do not cover civic education related subjects on a regular basis."[48]

In a sense, then, history and civics have lost out to what seemed like higher, or at least newer, priorities. It was less a decision to deemphasize civics and history as it was the inevitable result of choosing to emphasize other things instead. Keeping America competitive in international tests of reading and math and making certain that the US could compete globally in science and technology took precedence over providing the sort of civic education that would keep the American republic healthy and intact.

The Federal Government Has Also Retreated from Civic Education

Even though the federal role in civics is secondary to those of the state and local governments, the federal government has historically carried out certain responsibilities in the field. Federal funding for civic education, especially targeted toward teacher preparation, has declined precipitously in recent years. In 2010, for example, federal funding for civics amounted to approximately $150 million per year, but, by 2019, that had declined to a mere $5 million.[49] One expert has put this into stark terms by noting that we now spend $54 per student per year on STEM education and only 5 cents per student on civics.

---

[48] Ibid.

[49] "Inspired to Serve," National Commission on Military, National and Public Service, March 16, 2020, https://inspire2serve.gov/reports/final-report.

Another federal responsibility of increasing importance is the national testing program on key subjects. The National Assessment of Educational Progress (NAEP) was mandated by Congress, and its test results are aggregated and reported by state so that they can track how students are performing. Certain subjects—especially math, reading, and science—are tested and reported frequently: at least once in the elementary years (fourth grade), then during middle school (eighth grade), and finally high school (twelfth grade). These are the kind of tests around which the culture of testing, including the vast amount of time preparing for administering the tests, has been built. Estimates indicate that students spend as many as twenty days per school year taking standardized tests and another twenty-six days preparing for them.[50]

In contrast, subjects such as civics and history are tested comparatively rarely, which delivers a message to schools, students, and teachers about their lack of importance. The NAEP tests on US history and civics/government are only administered once, in the eighth grade. Besides underscoring their lack of importance, this also leaves us bereft of information about how students are doing in these subjects in elementary school and high school. In that sense, the terrible test scores we know about in eighth grade may not even tell the full story of how little civics and history students actually know across the grade span.

---

[50] Erik Robelen, "Testing and Test Prep: How Much Is Too Much?," Education Writers Association, June 3, 2016, https://www.ewa.org/blog-educated-reporter/testing-and-test-prep-how-much-too-much.

The Neglect of Knowledge in Schools, including Civic Knowledge

There is a deeper neglect in education that has also diminished civic education. Two books published in 2019 note this problem of neglect of knowledge as a primary goal of education. E. D. Hirsch Jr., an influential expert in education, published *Why Knowledge Matters*, exploring why American students have shown dramatic drops in their academic scores, especially between 1960 and 1980.[51] He concluded that the "achievement gap is chiefly a knowledge and a language gap," noting "it can be greatly ameliorated by knowledge-based schooling."[52] As Hirsch developed his argument, he claimed that as high-stakes reading tests became central to schooling, they replaced knowledge of history and culture with reading skills instead. Some educational theorists decided that they could develop in students the skills of making inferences or finding the main idea without bothering with in-depth knowledge.[53]

Hirsch notes that some people have come to believe that reading skills can be taught as well with *Tyler Makes Pancakes!* or *Stupendous Sports Stadiums* as with a biography of Abraham Lincoln. If this theory is followed, it would mean that young people no longer build a base of literary and historical knowledge as they once did. When they finally come to the one civics course that remains in the curriculum in high school, they

---

[51] E. D. Hirsch Jr., Why Knowledge Matters: Rescuing Our Children from Failed Educational Theories (Massachusetts: Harvard Education Press, 2019), 6.

[52] Ibid., 1–2.

[53] Ibid., 19.

lack any sort of context for the subject matter. They "lack the knowledge," Hirsch argues, "to understand the mature language of newspapers, textbooks and political speeches."[54] The civics course, then, feels simply like a boring exercise in memorizing facts and developing knowledge to which students have never been exposed.

Education journalist Natalie Wexler made a similar case in her 2019 book, *The Knowledge Gap*.[55] Like Hirsch, Wexler argues that some theorists have concluded that reading is "a set of skills to be taught completely disconnected from content."[56] In this view, students must spend their time "learning to read" before they can progress to "reading to learn." Wexler describes this starkly as a "content-free curriculum," which would leave high school students without sufficient knowledge of history to be able to understand the American system in their civics course.[57] In that sense, she says, "a high school civics course may be too little and too late."[58] Ironically, Wexler added, this approach has not led to an improvement in reading test scores either.[59]

Unfortunately, traditional means to acquire civic knowledge has, from many quarters, been criticized as an outmoded and boring approach to teaching civics, making it even more difficult to strengthen and revive it. Then US secretary of education Arne Duncan described this problem as "old school" civics, a

---

54 Ibid., 20.
55 Natalie Wexler, *The Knowledge Gap: The Hidden Cause of America's Broken Education System—and How to Fix It* (New York: Avery, 2019).
56 Ibid., 6.
57 Ibid., 127.
58 Ibid., 10.
59 Ibid., 9.

form of education that, he said, "can seem antiquated."[60] In an unfortunate reference, he called this "your grandmother's civics," prompting him to advocate instead for the approach called "action civics" (which will be examined in detail in chapter two).

This sort of criticism will help insure that civic knowledge is not only dead but also properly buried. Indeed, it is lazy to suggest that teaching knowledge is boring, so let's teach something more entertaining. Great teachers around the country know that's not true! Engaging students in learning has always been one of the biggest challenges in the classroom. The answer, as we shall see from looking at effective teachers, is not to give up on teaching civic knowledge, but to do a better job of it, engaging students in the learning process.

We Have Neglected Teacher Preparation and Development in Civic Education

The two essential elements for improving civic education are the time spent in class learning the subject and the proper preparation and development of great teachers. Unfortunately, we are doing little better helping teachers offer civics courses than we are managing the precipitous decline in time spent on the task.

---

[60] Arne Duncan, "Secretary Arne Duncan's Remarks at 'For Democracy's Future' Forum at the White House," DemocracyU, January 10, 2012, https://democracyu.wordpress.com/2012/01/20/secretary-arne-duncans-remarks-at-for-democracys-future-forum-at-the-white-house/.

The Sad State of History and Civics Textbooks

Of course, teachers cannot be effective without excellent teaching tools, and that has fundamentally meant textbooks. Unfortunately, textbooks in the field of civic education have often ranged from being boring to biased.

Let's begin by examining a textbook in use in both high schools and colleges: Howard Zinn's *A People's History of the United States*. Zinn, a history professor, was described in his obituary as "proudly, unabashedly radical,"[61] and his book certainly reflected that. Indeed, it was initially received as a kind of supplemental text, challenging some of the triumphal myths of American history, but over time, it has become much more broadly accepted. Stanford University education professor Sam Wineburg has said that it "has arguably had a greater influence on how Americans understand their past than any other book."[62]

Zinn starts right in with Christopher Columbus, whom he maintains is not an explorer and discoverer but a greedy murderer whose message to native Indians was to show him the gold. The discovery of the New World, according to Zinn, was not about pioneering a new frontier but rather a narrative about the destruction of indigenous peoples. The founding of the United States from the American Revolution in 1776 through the adoption of the Constitution in 1787 was a myth invented by the upper class and sold to the common man. According to Zinn, the Constitution's checks and balances served no more noble

---

[61]   Michael Powell, "Howard Zinn, Historian, Is Dead At 87," New York Times, January 28, 2010, https://www.nytimes.com/2010/01/29/us/29zinn.html.

[62]   Sam Wineburg, "Undue Certainty: Where Howard Zinn's A People's History Falls Short," American Educator (Winter 2012–14): 26–34.

purpose than maintaining order on behalf of the wealthy few over the many who were poor.

Zinn's effort to rewrite American history continued right on through the twentieth century. He noted favorably socialists and others who extended the "ideas of Karl Marx...that people might cooperatively use the treasures of the earth to make life better for everyone, not just a few."[63] Even the Progressives and Franklin Roosevelt's New Deal did not go far enough for Zinn, who also claimed that World War II was about "advancing the imperial interests of the United States" and that even the liberal presidency of John F. Kennedy in the early 1960s continued policies of unequal wealth distribution. Zinn summarized the fifty years prior to his book as "capitalistic encouragement of enormous fortunes alongside desperate poverty, a nationalistic acceptance of war and preparations for war."[64]

By his own terms, Howard Zinn sought to write a history that is on behalf of the executed or marginalized, not "on the side of the executioners."[65] Needless to say, the Zinn textbook has caused much confusion and consternation for teachers, students, and the public alike. If students come to accept Zinn's account, he will have succeeded in undercutting any sense of pride in their nation they might have developed. As Gordon Lloyd, an expert on the American founding, has said, "It's hard to love an ugly founding," which of course is exactly what Zinn has offered his readers. Much of the rancorous political debate we now see over American history is rooted in Zinn's controversial

---

[63] Howard Zinn, A People's History of the United States: 1492-Present (New York: Harper Perennial Modern Classics, 2005), 339.

[64] Ibid., 563.

[65] Ibid., 10.

but influential textbook. It is not going too far to hold Zinn at least partly responsible for politicizing American history and civics and eroding the sense of informed patriotism such studies could otherwise encourage in the young.

Less well known about the politics of textbooks is the fact that the same history and civics textbooks often publish different versions in order to satisfy the political and cultural requirements in different states. Textbooks in California and Texas, for example, tell different stories about subjects such as race, immigration, gender, sexuality, and the role of religion.[66] Once authors (often academics) prepare a textbook, publishers then go through the extensive process of revising the books for sale in various states, which have their own standards. Dueling textbooks tell their own distinctive stories.

Between the attacks on the teaching of civics as boring and antiquated and the politicized approach of Howard Zinn and his progeny, too many civics textbooks and teaching materials are simply not up to the task. Too often poorly prepared, teachers are sent into the classroom with inadequate tools. It is a recipe for civic disaster, which, as our test scores and other signs indicate, is exactly what we have reaped.

---

[66] Dana Goldstein, "Two States. Eight Textbooks. Two American Stories.," New York Times, January 12, 2020
https://www.nytimes.com/interactive/2020/01/12/us/texas-vs-california-history-textbooks.html.

Hyperpartisan Politics Have Stymied Teaching History and Civics

Writing of a different time, Thomas Mann said, "Everything is politics." Unfortunately, this rings true today, and we should not be surprised that politics has reared its ugly head in the teaching of American history and civics. Political battles at all levels—federal, state, school, and within families—have become a major distraction to the teaching of civics and history, erecting a roadblock to the sort of progress we should be making.

Perhaps the good news is that civic education is now beginning to be part of the public debate and receiving the increased attention that it deserves. Though not without criticism, a new civics "roadmap," funded by the National Endowment for the Humanities and developed by three hundred scholars and practitioners, has been released.[67] This document seeks to foster both improvement in civic education and the use of civics to bridge some of America's deep divisions. Meanwhile, in Washington, DC, a $1 billion Civics Secures Democracy Act was introduced with bipartisan support.[68] The Fordham Institute published a 370-page report grading all the states in civics and history education (the results were not promising).[69]

The primary activity at the state level—where a civic education curriculum should be established—has been heavily politicized, with battles over particular approaches to civics

---

[67] "We have created a roadmap for excellence in history and civics," Educating for American Democracy, https://www.educatingforamericandemocracy.org/.

[68] https://www.congress.gov/bill/117th-congress/senate-bill/879To [URL Inactive]

[69] Stern et al., "The State of State Standards."

and history such as Critical Race Theory (CRT) and the 1619 Project. Critical Race Theory argues that the teaching of US history and civics must start from the assumption that America is systemically racist. The 1619 Project argues that the coming of slavery to the continent in 1619, not the American Revolution of 1776, was the real founding of the country, and everything must be taught from that starting point.

Not only are scholars debating these ideas, but state legislatures have taken up the questions by proposing bans on the teaching of these ideas.[70] All these controversies tie up state legislatures in further political battles rather than in the more positive and long-term work of setting appropriate history and civics curricula and requirements for states.

There Is No Major Initiative for Better Civic Education

At certain points in recent decades, there has been a strongly felt need and a major push in favor of reforming and improving K–12 education. When the Soviet Union successfully launched Sputnik in 1957, it not only prompted President John F. Kennedy to announce a major initiative to reach the moon, but it also led to immediate calls for improvement in American math and science education. One panelist at a Harvard University program correctly called Sputnik a wake-up

---

[70] Maggie Hicks, "Experts fear ban on critical race theory could harm civic education," The Fulcrum, August 12, 2021, https://thefulcrum.us/civic-ed/critical-race-theory-civic-ed.

call and a "focusing event" that led, a year later, to the passage of the National Defense Education Act.[71]

Similarly, a concern that test scores of US students were falling behind those of other industrialized nations stirred up experts and resulted in a major national report published in 1983: *A Nation at Risk*. The subtitle of the report, *The Imperative for Educational Reform*, captured the call to action. The report observed falling SAT test scores from 1963 to 1980, noting a "rising tide of mediocrity" in American education. Using examples that might parallel the civic education crisis today, experts observed that 40 percent of seventeen-year-olds could not draw inferences from written material, and only one-third could solve mathematical problems requiring several steps. The report led to a number of reforms at all educational levels.

Once again, in the early 2000s, experts noted that American students were falling behind their international peers in science and math. This led to a competitive concern that the US economy would not be able to keep up, because our students were not ready for jobs in various fields of science and technology. As a result, improving STEM became the call of the day, with billions of dollars invested. The STEM movement has now become one of the primary forces in American education.

Unfortunately, there is not yet a similar movement for civic education. Although sagging test scores suggest major gaps in civic education, there is no call comparable to Sputnik, *A Nation at Risk*, or STEM to address the problem. A few bills, accompanied by speeches from their sponsors,

---

[71] Alvin Powell, "How Sputnik changed U.S. education," The Harvard Gazette, October 11, 2007, https://news.harvard.edu/gazette/story/2007/10/how-sputnik-changed-u-s-education/.

have been introduced in Congress to improve civics, but these bills just sit in committees gathering dust. Perhaps, because the issue is not one of international competitiveness as it was in these other movements, there is not yet enough momentum for change. Yet our nation's very republic is at risk if we fail to prepare students to understand and lead it, so surely the emergency is at least as great as in those other times when educational reform was demanded.

Surprisingly, there hasn't been a major philanthropist coming forward to invest massively in civic education. We live in a time when billionaire philanthropists are able to move more rapidly than governments or movements to address serious problems—Bill Gates and his foundation's efforts to address world health challenges being a prime example. Other more grassroots organizations, such as Rotary International, have mobilized clubs all over the world to eradicate polio and great progress has been made. Philanthropists have responded to the crises of the day with major support for COVID-19 relief, Black Lives Matter, and so on. With the exception of a few foundations, however, no major philanthropist has championed the cause of civic education in a bold way.

One of the early voices expressing the need for better civic education was President Ronald Reagan in his farewell message in 1989. Reagan was speaking before new curricular priorities from No Child Left Behind and STEM education had begun crowding civic education out of the heart of the curriculum, so his emphasis was more on the content of civic education and the need for parents to lead the charge. "All great change in America begins at the dinner table," Reagan said. His concern was that a renewed patriotism in the country would not last unless it was rooted in knowledge, and so he called for "an informed patriotism" beginning with parents and the family. This phrase alone—"an informed patriotism"—is a major contribution to the civics cause, capturing both the need for knowledge but, ultimately, also a love of country as an appropriate goal for civic education.

Other important voices began to join the chorus. US Supreme Court Justice Sandra Day O'Connor was among the early prophets of the need for better civic education. Soon after retiring from the Supreme Court in 2006, O'Connor made it known that strengthening civic education and engagement would be her priority going forward. Her goal was that people gain a better understanding of the Constitution and America's unique system of government and that they find ways to make an active contribution. In addition to her personal leadership, O'Connor's civics legacy was the creation of a new organization, iCivics, in 2009. iCivics has taken the lead in developing games and other online tools to help engage children in the study of civics.

Rather than a groundswell of interest and concern, expressions of the need for better civic education was more like a trickle. It was as if one person and then another awakened to the danger of weak civic education. Retired supreme court justice David Souter began working on civic education in his home state of New Hampshire and delivered a major national address about it. The actor Richard Dreyfuss weighed in. Following the election of Donald Trump as president in 2016, liberals began to conclude that there must be something wrong with the system. The riots at the US Capitol in 2021 led many to wonder whether poor civic education was part of our republic's problem. But no major champion arose. No billionaire offered major funding.

Indeed, even as people were awakening to the problem, strong winds continued to blow against civic education. The federal government essentially stopped funding civic education through its teacher training programs, turning instead to provide massive funding to STEM education. States and school districts reduced their classes in humanities and the social sciences, including civics, in response to the demands of No Child Left Behind for more emphasis and testing in reading and math. STEM education swept the country and the school curriculum, leaving less money and room for the teaching of civics.

Perhaps this book could play some small role in helping to foster a stronger grassroots movement for civic education that could catch fire. As Thomas Sowell pointed out in his book *Intellectuals and Society*, intellectuals play the increasingly important role of creating "a climate of opinion" or a "vision" that serves as a "general framework for the way particular issues and events...are perceived" and then "discussed and ultimately acted upon by those with political power."[72] In other words, rather than lobbying political leaders or even philanthropists directly— they are pitched ideas all the time—perhaps the way to get there is to build a climate of opinion, a bandwagon of energy about the civic education problem and the need to solve it.

---

[72] Thomas Sowell, Intellectuals and Society, (New York: Basic Books, 2009), 282, 284.

CHAPTER TWO

Making the Crisis Worse: The History and Civics Wars

The twentieth-century writer Thomas Mann could have been speaking of our day when he said, "Everything is politics." Many of us can remember a time when your politics was simply which candidate you voted for or which political party you identified with. At the most, it might have been one of several ways of describing a person's loyalties and affiliations including ethnicity, religion, home state, schools attended, and so forth. A well-known saying held that the two topics you did not discuss in polite company were politics and religion, intended to prevent even the possibility that such topics could lead to arguments or controversies. Not so today—everything is politics, and heated politics at that.

Now consumers may consider not just price and quality when making a purchasing decision, but also the politics of the company that is selling the product. Many people boycott My Pillow or don't eat at Chick-fil-A, for example, because of the owners' beliefs. A ballot proposition is no longer just something you vote for or against—on some issues, people seek out the names of everyone giving money to support or oppose a measure in order to shun them or boycott their business. Corporate presidents may lose their jobs for political incorrectness or be disciplined over political expressions on social media (which have certainly fueled the fires of political controversy to burn bright and hot).

Sports used to be an escape from politics and other cares of the world, but not these days. Colin Kaepernick brought politics into the spotlight in the NFL when he made a political statement by kneeling rather than standing during the national anthem. Soon, that practice spread throughout the teams of the NFL, NBA, and other sports. Basketball players began wearing political labels and slogans on their uniforms as part of the Black Lives Matter movement. Major League Baseball removed its annual All-Star game from Atlanta over voting rights legislation in Georgia. The primary owner of the San Francisco Giants was roundly attacked because his more conservative politics did not play well in the more liberal Bay Area.

The recent COVID-19 pandemic is a microcosm of the problem. Soon enough, wearing a mask became not a question of health, but a political statement. Whether or not you were vaccinated was often reduced to a political question. Conservative states sought to prevent widespread closures of schools and businesses, while more liberal states accepted such limitations more readily. The divide between red and blue states, an expression not known in the political world fifty years ago, became all the more evident. Rather than people pulling together to battle a worldwide pandemic, they pulled apart over its politics.

Politics in Civic Education

It should not be surprising, then, that politics has also invaded the field of civic education. Seemingly overnight, important elements of civics and US history have become major battlegrounds from Washington, DC, to state capitals, and within communities, from boards of education to school classrooms. In Washington, there has been controversy over what was once thought to be a popular legislative effort to provide more financial support for civic education. As is often the case, however, help from Washington usually comes with strings attached and those provisions have stirred up debate, stalling the bills in committees.

In the majority of state capitals, bills have been introduced, and many have passed, banning the teaching of specific ideas—especially Critical Race Theory and the 1619 Project—by withholding funding to schools that allow the teaching of these controversial approaches. Since K–12 education is still largely a local matter, school board meetings and classrooms have also heated up over what civics and history can be taught and even what books may be held by their libraries.

All this represents a major change from the origins of American civic education through a post–World War II consensus in favor of teaching a patriotic, pro-American brand of civics and history. The Founders saw educating for citizenship as a fundamental purpose of schooling,[73] but the modern development of civic education dates to the 1830s, when Horace Mann led the Common Schools Movement.[74] The goal was to create both good citizens and good persons, including a loyalty to America and her ideals.[75] It was also thought to be a way to assimilate America's immigrants.[76] This kind of patriotic civic education maintained a wide consensus through both the First and Second World Wars and usually involved multiple courses in the subject.

Beginning with the 1980 publication of Howard Zinn's textbook, *A People's History of the United States*, that consensus came undone. As we saw previously, Zinn argued that the American story should be told from the point of view of oppressed peoples, essentially rewriting the whole of American history and civics, from Christopher Columbus and the Founders right on through the present day. Initially thought of as an alternative understanding of history and civics and therefore a supplementary text, Zinn's book gained wide acceptance in high school and college classrooms, becoming a best-selling text. From that point forward, the content of US history and civics courses came under debate so that, by today, it is a heated controversy at all levels of education.

---

[73] Michael T. Rogers, "A Meta-History of Formal Civic Education: An Episodic History To Be Repeated?," in Michael T. Rogers and Donald M. Gooch (eds), Civic Education in the Twenty-First Century (Lanham: Lexington Books, 2015), 6-7.

[74] "History of Civics Education in the United States," Research 4SC, https://research4sc.org/history-of-civics-education-in-the-united-states/.

[75] Ibid.

[76] Charles N. Quigley, "Civic Education: Recent History, Current Status, and the Future," ABA Symposium, February 25–26, 1999.

When everything is political, it becomes difficult to address normal pedagogical concerns. Rather than providing funding, Washington, DC, can be easily caught up in the nature of civic education to be funded. Instead of focusing on how much civics to require and in what grades, state legislatures have become wrapped up in whether specific approaches to civics and history may or may not be taught. School boards and schools have become hotbeds of controversy rather than objective sources of teaching and learning. Textbook adoption has become more difficult with separate versions of most texts published to suit the particularities of the several states—both red and blue. All this makes improving civic education considerably more difficult.

In order to sort out the politics of civic education, some additional analysis and understanding is required.

Political Battleground: The Players

To the extent that civic education has become a political battleground, it helps to understand the combatants. One group, perhaps best identified as conservatives or traditionalists, essentially identify themselves with the Founders. Their view is that civic education has its roots and finds its purpose in the American Founding. With the Declaration of Independence as the philosophical founding document, the Constitution created the political structures and processes to deliver on those promises. Civic education, then, is to steep our future citizens in the what, how, and why of our constitutional republic, building in students a respect and love of country as the Founders established it. A good civics education to conservatives or traditionalists would be faithful to the Founding, helping students understand the why, how, and what of everything from "all men are created equal" in the Declaration to the representative government, checks and balances, and separation of power established by the Constitution.

A second view of civic education essentially grows out of the Progressive Era of the late nineteenth and early twentieth centuries. The progressives—especially figures like Woodrow Wilson—felt that in many ways, America had been ill-founded and needed to be corrected. Progressive thinkers, such as Herbert Croly and Charles Beard, argued that what the Founders established might have worked for a small population enjoying unlimited land, but with the Industrial Revolution and people living more closely together in cities, the American way was no longer fair to everyone. The federal government, these progressives claimed, needed to take a much more active and regulatory role in the economy, in labor policies, welfare, and the like. Checks and balances merely served to prevent the government from doing what needed to be done. Business barons needed to be opposed and more policies needed to be developed to help what Franklin Roosevelt came to call "the forgotten man."

Proponents of this progressive view—from Howard Zinn in 1980 to the Progressive Movement of the 2020s—would teach a very different brand of civic education, emphasizing social justice, maintaining that the American system was built on slavery and exposing its unfairness. These claims about social justice and civil rights need to be at the heart of civic education, progressives claim, not technicalities and governmental limitations such as checks and balances and separation of power.

In his book *The Conservative Sensibility*,[77] George Will argues that this "founding versus progressive" argument is what is dividing Americans as a whole today. What conservatives seek to conserve is "the American founding"[78]; it was understood by the Founders that "inequality in social outcomes was inevitable and by no means inherently deplorable" and the normal operation of a free society would "naturally produce inequalities."[79] The progressives, however, found these inequalities precisely what government should seek to correct, not only through education but also with economic and social programs.

The players in the politics of civic education are precisely those in the larger body politic: conservatives, or traditionalists, seeking to preserve the Founding on one hand, and progressives, or liberals, whose goal is to correct the inequalities and injustices of the Founding on the other. Progressives would undertake radical surgery on the American story to show the serious errors of slavery and social injustice and their consequences from the beginning right on through today. Conservatives might agree that such injustices have existed, but they resist the notion that these should change the entire narrative of American history and civics, noting that the American system set into motion and allowed for the ongoing correction of errors and unfairness. These liberals and conservatives fight their battles at every level, from schools to school boards to state legislatures and beyond. As such, they and the battles they choose to fight greatly

---

[77] George F. Will, The Conservative Sensibility (New York: Hachette Books, 2019).

[78] Ibid., xvii.

[79] Ibid., 53–54.

complicate any kind of bipartisan effort to strengthen civic education. Like so much in our hyperpartisan political world, the *politics* of civic education becomes the central debate, not how to strengthen it and increase its role in the education of young people.

The play-by-play of the civic education political wars looks something like this: The conservative, or traditional, view of civics and history has come under attack by Zinn and the progressives. With the strong leftward tilt in American colleges and universities, especially in the social sciences, new ideas such as Critical Race Theory and the 1619 Project are created by academics to change the teaching of history and civics in order to rewrite the American narrative. Conservatives have greater power in the political realm than in academia, so they respond in the way they can: passing policies in school boards and bills in state legislatures banning the teaching of these progressive ideas. This political battle then dominates the public debate about civic education rather than the more pragmatic issues of how much to invest in civic education, or how many courses to require, or how American students score in their knowledge of civics. It will be difficult to address these educational issues on the ground level with all the political bomb-throwing and attacks filling the air.

Political Battleground: The Issues

The 1619 Project, Critical Race Theory, and ethnic studies are specific initiatives that advance the progressive approach to civics—each of which deserves attention.

The 1619 Project, conceived and written by reporter Nikole Hannah-Jones and published in the *New York Times Magazine* in August 2019, seeks to reframe the founding of the country as the time when slaves first came to the continent rather than the traditional founding dates of 1776, the Declaration of Independence and American Revolution, and 1787, the signing of the Constitution. In that sense, the 1619 Project would establish the economic institution of slavery—widely practiced around the world at the time—as the real founding story, not the principles of freedom and equality proclaimed by the Declaration and the unique political system established by the Constitution.

The 1619 Project sought not to simply add a clearer and stronger understanding of slavery to the American narrative, but to pursue the much bolder agenda of rewriting the American story with slavery as its origin. As explained in its introductory essay, it "aims to reframe the country's history by placing the consequences of slavery and the contributions of black Americans at the very center of our national narrative." As Hannah-Jones wrote in her opening essay, "No aspect of the country that would be formed here has been untouched by the years of slavery that followed." Such a broad claim sets the stage for a major political battle, since the goal is not to add to the American narrative but to radically revise it, leading to the all-or-nothing approach of the new progressive history and civics initiatives, as well as the conservative response.

The 1619 Project immediately undertook an effort to reach school teachers and embed itself in the history and civics curricula. The Pulitzer Center published curricular materials to enable teachers to bring the 1619 Project into the classroom with widespread adoption and use.[80] A report from the Center's website in October 2020 showed that four thousand schools in all fifty states had adopted these materials, and doubtless thousands more have joined the effort since then.[81] More recently, Penguin Random House joined in the educational effort, following its publication of Nikole Hannah-Jones's newer book on the subject. This effort to redefine the Founding and restate the American story has gained significant attention and traction.

One conservative response to the 1619 Project was former president Donald Trump's formation of a federal 1776 Commission late in his administration. The Commission's report sought to reaffirm 1776 as the real and proper founding of the nation.[82] It is a sign of the highly politicized times in which we live when a *New York Times* report can call forth a federal commission to respond. So now, we have dueling reports about our nation's founding.

Also influential, however, have been political efforts to block the teaching of the 1619 Project in schools of particular states. With their greater political strength, especially at the state level, Republicans have introduced bills in more than half of state legislatures seeking to block teaching of the 1619 Project, among

---

[80] Naomi Schaeffer Riley, "'The 1619 Project' Enters American Classrooms," Education Next, last updated May 28, 2020, https://www.educationnext. org/1619-project-enters-american-classrooms-adding-new-sizzle-slavery-significant-cost/.

[81] Pauline Werner, "Educators Share Resources and Insights from 'The 1619 Project' in the Classroom," Pulitzer Center, October 13, 2020, https://pulitzercenter.org/blog/educators-share-resources-and-insights-1619-project-classroom.

[82] The President's Advisory 1776 Commission, The 1776 Report, January 2021, https://trumpwhitehouse.archives.gov/wp-content/uploads/2021/01/The-Presidents-Advisory-1776-Commission-Final-Report.pdf.

other topics they find objectionable in history and civic education. Such bills have passed in Tennessee, Texas, and Idaho and have been introduced in other states with mixed results. The Florida School Board has also banned the teaching of the 1619 Project. Arkansas and Mississippi passed bills that call the 1619 Project "a racially divisive and revisionist account." Iowa, more directly, claimed that it "attempts to deny or obfuscate the fundamental premises upon which the United States was founded." These states enforce these bans by reducing funding to schools that persist in teaching the 1619 Project. Proponents of the 1619 Project have fought back so that all sides are now heavily engaged in this matter.

Meanwhile, a new book expanding on the 1619 Project has been published, and it reveals more fully the political agenda of the 1619 Project.[83] In the concluding chapter of the book, Nikole Hannah-Jones calls for "a vast social transformation produced by the adoption of bold national policies." As the *Washington Post* book critic, Carlos Lozada, wrote of the book, "And so the *New York Times'* 1619 Project is now enlisted in the service of a policy agenda and political worldview."[84] In fact, Lozada's book review—"The 1619 Project started as history. Now it's also a political program."—is titled to indicate the political nature of the 1619 Project. Clearly, these political battles will continue, and doubtless accelerate. Sadly, adults have brought their ideological and political battles rather than history and civics into

---

[83] Nikole Hannah-Jones, The 1619 Project: A New Origin Story (New York: One World, 2021).

[84] Carlos Lozada, "The 1619 Project started as history. Now it's also a political program.," Washington Post, November 19, 2021, https://www.washingtonpost.com/outlook/2021/11/19/1619-project-book-history/.

their children's classrooms, and surely their education is not the better for it.

A closely related, and even larger, political battle has arisen over Critical Race Theory (CRT), which originated as a legal theory developed by a law professor, Kimberle Williams Crenshaw, forty years ago. She has described it as a way of seeing and understanding how racism develops and advances in a society.[85] It has been the subject of scholarly debate for decades about institutions and systems and the role they play in fostering racism in society and the law. CRT was not originally understood as a worldview, or even a single point of view, but more as an approach or a field of study on the question of whether racism was a natural or societal construct.

More recently, however, CRT has gained a major political profile in the history and civics education wars. It has become a political label used to describe and attack a broad range of ideas about social justice. In 2020, following the death of George Floyd, former president Donald Trump issued a memo demanding that federal agencies (and dollars) not be used to teach CRT because "it seeks to undercut our core values as Americans and drive division in our workforce."[86] It lumped CRT in with teaching about "white privilege" and other ideas about white racism.[87] With that memo, CRT

---

[85] Jacey Fortin, "Critical Race Theory: A Brief History," New York Times, November 8, 2021, https://www.nytimes.com/article/what-is-critical-race-theory.html.

[86] Russell Vought, Memorandum for the Heads of Executive Departments and Agencies, September 4, 2020, https://www.whitehouse.gov/wp-content/uploads/2020/09/M-20-34.pdf.

[87] Ibid.

entered the realm of administrative law and was therefore banned by the president from use in federal training.

Soon, school districts and states began to debate banning the teaching of CRT. In doing so, CRT was not understood as a field of academic study and debate about institutions and systems, but as a broader label for a set of ideas about racism and social justice. Conservatives found CRT a convenient and politically charged description for everything from Marxism to wokeism to race and gender theory. A conservative activist in the CRT political wars, Christopher Rufo, has pointed out that the label is useful because "its connotations are all negative to most middle class Americans, including racial minorities."[88]

As with the 1619 Project, conservative parents have gone to school boards and especially state legislatures in an effort to ban the teaching of CRT. The majority of states have now banned, or are considering banning, the teaching of CRT on the grounds that it creates divisiveness among social or racial classes of people.[89] Typical is the language in Tennessee House Bill 0623 seeking to ban any teaching that could lead a student to "feel discomfort, guilt, anguish or another form of psychological distress solely because of the individual's race or sex."

---

[88]   Benjamin Wallace-Wells, "How A Conservative Activist Invented The Conflict Over Critical Race Theory," The New Yorker, June 18, 2021, https://www.newyorker.com/news/annals-of-inquiry/how-a-conservative-activist-invented-the-conflict-over-critical-race-theory.

[89]   "Critical Race Theory Ban States," World Population Review, Updated April 2023, https://worldpopulationreview.com/state-rankings/states-that-have-banned-critical-race-theory.

Some debates address how teachers deal with issues, such as communism and current events,[90] with some bills banning the teaching of Howard Zinn's material and even anything against capitalism. (One bill reflected an ignorance of history when it said that one subject to be discussed by students was the debates between Abraham Lincoln and Frederick Douglass—of course, Lincoln debated Stephen Douglas instead.[91])

It is not overstating the matter to say that these arguments, and bills that dictate what teachers may or may not teach, are sweeping the country.

Some have suggested that what we have now is a culture war being waged on the back of our children's education. An article in the *Washington Post* concluded, "Political battles are now a central feature of education, leaving school boards, educators and students in the crosshairs of cultural warriors."[92] Parents of school students have been energized in such a way that politicians now view them as a political force to organize and engage in elections. For example, it is widely believed that Glenn Youngkin was elected Virginia's governor in 2021 on the

---

[90] Sarah Schwartz, "Who's Really Driving Critical Race Theory Legislation? An Investigation," Education Week, July 19, 2021, https://www.edweek.org/policy-politics/whos-really-driving-critical-race-theory-legislation-an-investigation/2021/07.

[91] Scott Jaschik, "Va. Legislator's Mistake in Taking on Critical Race Theory," Inside Higher Ed, January 17, 2022, https://www.insidehighered.com/quicktakes/2022/01/18/va-legislator%E2%80%99s-mistake-taking-critical-race-theory.

[92] Laura Meckler, "Public education is facing a crisis of epic proportions," Washington Post, January 30, 2022, https://www.washingtonpost.com/education/2022/01/30/public-education-crisis-enrollment-violence/.

strength of such issues,[93] providing a political roadmap for other candidates. If that is true, the politics of civic education will continue to expand from state legislatures and school boards to state and even federal political campaigns.

A related political controversy in the field of US history and civics is the ethnic studies movement. There has been a broad range of ethnic studies initiatives considered by state legislatures and school boards in recent years—spanning everything from teaching the history of certain ethnic groups, including a greater emphasis on indigenous peoples, to a broad array of gender and race-based rights.[94] The most comprehensive and controversial of these has been adopted in California, following a lengthy and highly politicized process. California became the first state to require an ethnic studies course in high school, beginning with the graduating class of 2029–30. The new law requires special emphasis on the history of African Americans, Latinos, Native Americans, and Asian Americans—groups all well represented in the state, in addition to other groups.[95] The adoption of a

93 Inez Stepman and Virginia Gentles, "What Glenn Youngkin Owes Virginia Parents," Newsweek, December 8, 2021, https://www.newsweek.com/what-glenn-youngkin-owes-virginia-parents-opinion-1656950.

94 Sylvia Kwon, Ethnic Studies Legislation: State Scan (Region 15 Comprehensive Center: CC Network, 2021), https://csaa.wested.org/wp-content/uploads/2021/03/ES-State-Scan-FINAL-v1.pdf.

95 John Fensterwald, "California becomes first state to require ethnic studies in high school," EdSource, October 8, 2021, https://edsource.org/2021/california-becomes-first-state-to-require-ethnic-studies-in-high-school/662219.

model curriculum followed years of intense debate and controversy, which is doubtless not fully settled even now.[96]

The Battlegrounds

These political battles over the teaching of US history and
civics are being played out on a number of battlefields, both
educational and governmental. On the governmental side,
the primary battlegrounds have been state legislatures and
state school boards as well as local school boards. As noted,
most state legislatures have considered and debated bills
about Critical Race Theory, the 1619 Project, ethnic studies,
and social justice. These matters are still being contested in
state capitals across the country. A number of conservative,
or so-called red, states have passed legislation along these
lines. One report indicates that in the first three weeks of
2022 alone, more than seventy such bills were introduced in
twenty-seven state legislatures, and 122 bills since January of
2021.[97] These bills often intensify the conflict between par-
ent groups and conservative legislators on one side and liberal
theorists and scholars on the other, with charges of racism
being hurled by both sides. State legislatures have become

---

[96] Mark Keierleber, "How California's Ethnic Studies Curriculum Got
Sucked Into the Culture Wars," The 74, April 15, 2021, https://www.
the74million.org/article/ethnic-studies-could-be-the-low-hanging-fruit-
of-american-education-reform-but-california-showed-how-creating-a-
curriculum-can-get-sucked-into-the-culture-wars/.

[97] Heidi Przybyla and Adam Edelman, "States weigh a raft of proposed laws
to limit race, sexuality lessons in schools," NBC News, January 28, 2022,
https://www.nbcnews.com/politics/politics-news/states-weigh-raft-pro-
posed-laws-limit-race-sexuality-lessons-schools-n1288108.

embroiled in the political controversy of what specifically can and cannot be taught or said by individual teachers in their classrooms.

Perhaps former House Speaker Tip O'Neil was right when he said, "All politics is local," because these highly politicized issues have made formerly pedestrian and decorous school board meetings into war zones. A brief report from the USC Rossier School of Education in August 2021 noted the increasing controversy and heated rhetoric about racial and social justice teaching in school board meetings.[98] There are heated debates, threats of harm to school board members, resignations, recalls, and lengthy meetings adjourned in controversy. One observer summarized school board meetings these days thusly: "Shoutings. Interruptions. Delays. Even police arrests."[99] While schools were already struggling through the pandemic, with controversies about masking and remote learning, school boards have been weighed down and often reduced to gridlock by these politicized debates.

One more battleground has emerged recently: school and public libraries. Reminiscent of book bannings decades ago, there is renewed controversy over whether certain books should be removed from school libraries because of their content. A number of school libraries across the country have removed books about racism and the Holocaust—some on the ground that they are "divisive," others because they were considered

[98] Brian Soika, "How school boards became lightning rods for controversy," USC Rossier School of Education, August 24, 2021, https://rossier.usc.edu/how-school-boards-became-lightning-rods-for-controversy/.

[99] Stephen Sawchuk, "Why School Boards Are Now Hot Spots for Nasty Politics," Education Week, July 29, 2021, https://www.edweek.org/leadership/why-school-boards-are-now-hot-spots-for-nasty-politics/2021/07.

too graphic in their depictions of violence.[100] The attacks come from both the Left and the Right, as books such as *To Kill a Mockingbird* are called into question. The American Library Association reported that an "unprecedented" 330 book challenges had been received.[101] Britten Follett, CEO of one of the largest book providers for schools, said, "The politicization of the topic is different from what I've seen in the past. It's being driven by legislation…by politicians… And in the end, the librarian, teacher or educator is getting caught in the middle."[102]

Finally, the classroom itself has become a battleground for politicized content controversy. In Virginia, for example, the governor established a "tip line" where people can report teachers for presenting "inherently divisive concepts."[103] Such a policy leaves teachers confused and uncertain about what they can or cannot teach. One teacher putting up a bulletin board for Black History Month asked, "What if I get reported to the governor for what I put up? It's horrifying."[104] This adds a layer of high-risk complexity to the already difficult tasks teachers face. Teachers

---

[100] Marilisa Jiménez Garcia, "Book Bans Are Targeting the History of Oppression," The Atlantic, February 2, 2022, https://www.theatlantic.com/family/archive/2022/02/maus-book-ban-tennessee-art-spiegelman/621453/.

[101] Elizabeth A. Harris and Alexandra Alter, "Book Ban Efforts Spread Across the U.S.," New York Times, January 30, 2022, https://www.nytimes.com/2022/01/30/books/book-ban-us-schools.html?referringSource=articleShare.

[102] Ibid.

[103] Michael Smolens, "Column: Legislation targets teachers for lessons on 'divisive' subjects, student confidentiality," The San Diego Union-Tribune, February 2, 2022, https://www.sandiegouniontribune.com/columnists/story/2022-02-02/column-intimidating-education-policies-target-teachers.

[104] Ibid.

now must also manage the increasingly political atmosphere and opinions of their own students and their families as they manage classroom discussion and learning. If, for example, they teach historical cases and examples, students may logically bring up similar and more politicized controversies of the current day. How can teachers allow such discussions without losing control of the heated politics that will be expressed? Creating "safe spaces" for such classroom discussions has become yet one more major challenge for history and civics teachers.

How We Can Reduce the Politicization of History and Civics

If we agree that politics has overtaken almost everything these days and that hyperpartisanship is the order of the day, how can this be addressed in civic education? In other words, if what we are facing is a heated politicization of nearly everything in our society, how can we try to fix that in just one corner—the civics classroom? It may well be the case that politicized civics and history will be almost inevitable unless, and until, we find some larger solutions to our politicized society and politics. Nevertheless, there may be a few steps that could lead toward some easing of the politicization of civics and history that are worth considering.

Perhaps an objective starting point would be a kind of structural analysis of what the various players should be doing about civic education rather than engaging in so much politics. A call to return to their fundamental purposes might be one way of reducing the political warfare and restoring a proper civic education.

Federal Funding

Take the federal government for example. Arguably, it has no role at all in civic education since K–12 education is, and should be, a state and local matter. Beginning with the 1965 Elementary and Secondary Education Act, however, Washington, DC, has long invested money in certain aspects of K–12 education, especially these days in STEM education. As stated in chapter one, there was significant federal support for teaching American history in the early 2000s—as much as $100–$150 million per year—but those grants were essentially cut from the budget and reduced to a mere $5 million by 2019.[105] As is widely reported, the federal government now spends $54 per student annually on STEM education but only 5 cents on civics.

The problem is that typically, when the federal government spends money on something, it also tries to exert some control over how it is spent. That question is on the table with the recently proposed Civics Secures Democracy Act introduced in Congress.[106] Although there have been discussions in Washington of providing as much as $1 billion for civics and history education, the details of a bill such as this indicate that the federal government may also seek to define the terms of some of these programs. For example, the Civics Secures Democracy Act indicates a need for "innovative, engaging curricula" that addresses not only civic knowledge but also "civic skills, civic dispositions and

---

[105] National Commission on Military, National and Public Service, *Inspired to Serve: The Final Report of the National Commission on Military, National, and Public Service* (DC: 2020), 16.

[106] "S.4384 – Civics Secures Democracy Act," 117th Congress (2021–2022), https://civxnow.org/wp-content/uploads/2022/06/CSD-Bill-Text-6-2022.pdf.

civic behaviors." The bill favors "community service" as well as "meaningful participation in school governance." This language touches on a number of debates about what is best in civic education and puts the federal thumb on the scale of civic education policy, which should be left to state and local governments. This bill, and some of its companions, have been stuck in committees with the details still under debate.

A far better federal investment, if one is to be made, would be to go back to funding teacher preparation and leaving the how and what of civic education to state and local authorities. As will be discussed in chapter five, one of the most important steps to be taken to address the civics crisis is better teacher education. Grants—to nonprofits and states—could accelerate our progress without excessive federal entanglement in how civics and history should be taught. Still, the best federal role is actually one of advocacy, not policy or even funding. We need leadership messages from Washington about the importance of civic education. If the federal government is to go beyond advocacy to funding, it should not engage itself in the politicized policy discussions that rightly belong to the states, school boards, and districts.

State Legislatures

As noted, conservative state legislatures are awash in bills to ban the teaching of concepts about racism and social justice deemed to be divisive or otherwise inappropriate, most prominently Critical Race Theory and the 1619 Project, while bills in progressive states like California, such as those on ethnic studies, seek to describe in detail new theories and ideas that must be taught. Of several things that could be said about these bills, foremost is that deciding the details of what is taught in individual classrooms is not really the purpose of a state legislature. The legislature's job is to set policy, leaving the particulars of how it is carried out to school boards and districts—and especially teachers themselves. What is most needed from state legislatures is more robust civic education requirements in school curricula: how much should be required, and in what grades must it be taught? Those are the central questions that should be front and center in our state legislatures, not which particular idea or theory should be taught. Notably, these key issues may well produce bipartisan agreement and progress, rather than the political controversies and stalemates now dominating our state legislatures.

Although it is understandable how these bills came about, they are not the best approach to the problem. Trying to stop everything bad that could be taught is an endless game that no one really wins. It is like the arcade game Whac-A-Mole in which every time moles pop up, the player must beat them down. But, like the moles, the educational theories and ideas keep coming. You never get them all. Legislatures are starting down a never-ending road of expanding their political work into all kinds of classroom matters.

A better long-term approach is to acknowledge that students will be exposed to both good and bad ideas in their education, and to build greater judgment and resilience in the students themselves. Using the analogy of a garden, there are both seeds and weeds in civic education. Although any gardener or farmer will want a good weed abatement program, you cannot spend all your time and energy attacking weeds. Eventually, you need to plant and cultivate crops that are sufficiently robust to resist weeds and pests. It makes sense, then, for legislatures to focus on planting more and better seeds in the civics garden rather than spending so much on the politics of pulling weeds. To borrow another traditional conservative philosophy, the best antidote to bad speech is good speech. As Supreme Court Justice Louis Brandeis famously put it in his opinion in *Whitney v. California* (1927): "If there be time to expose through discussion, the falsehoods and fallacies, to avert the evil by the processes of education, the remedy to be applied is more speech, not enforced silence." Even politically, the business of banning things has rarely been well received in America.

Classrooms

The role of the teacher, to be more fully explored in chapter five, involves selecting lessons and methods, teaching students the best material, and allowing students to discuss and decide tough issues for themselves. All of this is made more challenging by the highly politicized atmosphere surrounding nearly everything they do—unsure of what they can and cannot teach, challenged to manage politically charged issues and classrooms.

One way to do this is to be honest brokers of the content of American history and civics. While it is important that students have a positive understanding of the American system and its history, it is also crucial that they be exposed to mistakes and problems. The use of primary documents can be helpful in this kind of honest exchange of ideas, looking at periods of history in the terms of those who participated, and seeking to understanding their views. There is also an emerging literature on how to manage classrooms to allow students to learn how to have an honest exchange without losing control. It is crucial for teachers to enable students to see honest and rational exchanges of ideas—both in history and in the classroom. Teachers are not about choosing sides or ducking tough issues, but learning how to facilitate honest and deep study of American history and the tough issues facing the American system today. As all good teachers know, their role is not to indoctrinate, but to educate.

Conclusion

In the larger picture, it is important for leaders in the field to model some kind of consensus agenda for improving civic education, while allowing for freedom of speech and dissent. For example, there should be agreement on the need for more civic education with strong state requirements in elementary, middle, and high schools. It could take years to work through the curricular adjustments that would be needed, so that work needs to accelerate in state legislatures now. Politicians and social scientists should model how to disagree about history and civics without becoming irrational or creating hopeless divides. Again, the use of primary documents in the classroom can be a helpful tool for more objective teaching and learning.

One effort that merits attention seeks to identify a bipartisan "roadmap" of civic education throughout the school years. The Educating for American Democracy initiative was a huge undertaking funded by the National Endowment for the Humanities. In its own terms, it "convened a diverse and cross-ideological group of scholars and educators to create a Roadmap to

Educating for American Democracy."[107] It seeks to help states, school boards, and educators understand how to teach civics and history from kindergarten through high school. As we will outline later, we do not think that the roadmap by itself should guide civic education reform. Still, it was a useful effort to create some kind of bipartisan teaching and learning agenda for civics, and it is worthy of study by decision-makers.

As long as we live in a society where political conflict reigns, it will be difficult to exempt the teaching of history and civics from powerful political winds. Nevertheless, perhaps these suggestions will help move the teaching of civics into greater prominence and effectiveness, even while efforts are undertaken in other venues to try to lessen political partisanship and its corrosive effect.

---

[107] "We have created a roadmap," Educating for American Democracy.

CHAPTER THREE

Action Civics: The Wrong Solution to the Crisis

I f students are not learning a subject well enough, some say we need to change the way it is taught or even change what is taught. For example, if students are not learning math, let's change to a "new math," or if students cannot read well using phonics and sounding things out, let's employ a whole language curriculum instead. Surprise, surprise—the new approach is usually not a panacea, or even an improvement, and we often return to the old paths in the end.

Such is the story of what has come to be called "action civics." Instead of trying to do a better job of teaching American history and civics, proponents of action civics say "let's change what we teach—but still call it civics." Rather than employ the classroom and classic texts to learn the story of America and what responsibilities citizens should carry out, action civics says to get students out of the classroom and have them do civics—protesting, going on field trips, drafting bills, or helping in social service programs.

Students may enjoy action more than the classroom, but what are they really learning? And what additional problems might be created by deploying classes of students out in the political world?

The Origin and Development of Action Civics

The Mikva Challenge in Chicago is credited with coining the term "action civics" in 2007.[108] Notably, Mikva's stated goal is more civic engagement than civic education, seeking to "empower youth to become active and engaged citizens"[109] and in turn establishing habits of civic activity in future citizens. Mikva provides action civics training and curriculum to school districts around the country and runs programs in at least a dozen states.[110] With civic engagement—both now and later—as the real goal, any impact on civic education would be a byproduct.

Other organizations have taken up the action civics cause, with Generation Citizen joining the Mikva Challenge as the two largest organizations championing action civics. Generation Citizen states its mission in stronger and more specifically political terms, describing the problem it seeks to solve as "the reality

---

[108] Kelly Field, "Teaching 'action civics' engages kids — and ignites controversy," The Hechinger Report, August 1, 2021, https://hechingerreport. org/teaching-action-civics-engages-kids-and-ignites-controversy/.

[109] "Our Work," Mikva Challenge, https://mikvachallenge.org/our-work/.

[110] Field, "Teaching 'action civics.'"

of an unjust and unequal democracy."[111] Focusing on schools as the leverage point to address the problem, Generation Citizen says that civics education is "not prioritized" and, when taught, it "often fails to inspire and engage young people to work towards a robust, participatory, and inclusive democracy."[112] Their answer, then, is action civics, which is sometimes understood as teaching young people how to drive through the political process, a kind of driver's education course for civic engagement.

In her 2019 book *Building Better Citizens*, Holly Korbey reports that the Mikva Challenge and Generation Citizen had reached a combined thirty-four thousand students.[113] She also noted that some twenty other smaller organizations "are also offering action civics for schools."[114] Notable among these is the National Action Civics Collaborative, which seeks to share information among users of action civics. It titled its 2010 founding document, "Action Civics: A Declaration for Rejuvenating our Democratic Traditions."

Action civics has traveled under other names, which suggest some of its deeper roots. Conservative scholar Stanley Kurtz, an active opponent of the use of action civics in schools, points out that it is "sometimes called 'Civic Engagement,' 'New Civics,' or

---

[111] "Empowering Youth in Our Democracy Through Project-Based Civics," Generation Citizen, https://generationcitizen.org/about-us/the-problem/.
[112] Ibid.
[113] Holly Korbey, Building Better Citizens: A New Civic Education For All (Boulder, CO: Rowman & Littlefield, 2019), 127. ICivics, which reaches millions of students, also incorporates elements of action civics in its work.
[114] Ibid.

'Project-Based Civics.'"[115] Critics point out that with labels such as these, action civics seeks to identify itself as growing out of the more acceptable and less controversial base of volunteerism or service learning.[116]

Actually, three different ideas, including action civics, are being lumped together by some conservatives in a pushback against progressive change of history and civics in the schools. Critical Race Theory, the 1619 Project, and action civics are often joined together under the broader, and most controversial term: CRT. Pedagogically, action civics is different from the other two. Critical Race Theory and the 1619 Project teach definite ideas about systemic racism and slavery that many wish to block from classrooms. Action civics, on the other hand, is more in the nature of a method of teaching than a set of beliefs.

Is Action Civics Actually Civics at All?

Because of the decline in historical and civic knowledge, some people have felt free to trade in the old civics for something new—namely action civics. The question we must ask, then, is

---

[115] Stanley Kurtz, "'Action Civics' Replaces Citizenship With Partisanship," The American Mind, January 26, 2021, https://americanmind.org/memo/action-civics-replaces-citizenship-with-partisanship/.

[116] David Randall, Making Citizens: How American Universities Teach Civics, National Association of Scholars, January 2017, https://www.nas.org/storage/app/media/Reports/Making%20Citizens/NAS_makingCitizens_fullReport.pdf. See also: Peter Wood and David Randall, "Forcing Kids To Push Leftist Causes Is Not Civics No Matter How Many Think Tanks Say Otherwise," The Federalist, August 2, 2021, https://thefederalist.com/2021/08/02/forcing-kids-to-push-leftist-causes-is-not-civics-no-matter-how-many-think-tanks-say-otherwise/.

whether action civics is really effective at teaching civic education. Or, to put it another way, is action civics really civics at all, or is it something else entirely?

Critics of action civics make the case that, in actuality, it does not teach students civics at all. As Peter Wood, president of the National Association of Scholars, said of action civics, "It has the feel-good, reassuring word 'civics' in there, but it is actually a kind of anti-civics."[117] Another critic, John Sailer, argues that "it doesn't teach civics in any meaningful sense."[118] What, then, does action civics teach, if not civics, and why do some people feel a need to turn in that direction?

One view is that the old civics is simply boring and that the purpose of action civics is to engage students and make the subject more interesting. Viewed in that light, traditional history and civics is seen as simply memorizing a lot of information about the government and how it works—a rather limited view of civics, indeed. This, then, is denigrated, as former secretary of education Arne Duncan put it, as "your grandmother's civics."[119] Indeed, the National Action Civics Collaborative has attacked "traditional civic education" as "boring and ineffective" in its focus on the "basics of our political system."[120] This so-called

[117] Peter W. Wood, "Save America From Action Civics," RealClearEducation, March 22, 2021, https://www.realcleareducation.com/articles/2021/03/22/save_america_from_action_civics_110550.html.

[118] John D. Sailer, "The 'Action Civics' Bait-and-Switch," American Greatness, June 18, 2021, https://amgreatness.com/2021/06/18/the-action-civics-bait-and-switch/.

[119] Arne Duncan, "The Next Generation of Civics Education," Remarks at the iCivics "Educating for Democracy in a Digital Age" Conference, March 29, 2011.

[120] Adam Meyerson, "Challenges and Opportunities in Civic Education," Speech, April 11, 2019.

boring approach to teaching civics needs to be replaced, proponents argue, by action civics to get the kids more engaged and involved.

A broader understanding of the purpose of action civics is that it is simply one step away from teaching civic knowledge to teaching civic skills and activism instead. Rather than learning the story of America, why the republic was founded, and how it works, the purpose of action civics is to get students involved in doing something about its current direction. Proponents of the new civics (including action civics) speak of these goals as developing skills, habits, and civic dispositions rather than civic knowledge. It is about doing, not learning; it prioritizes action, not knowledge. It seems fair for critics to ask, then, to what extent does action civics even qualify as civic education? As longtime education expert Chester E. Finn Jr. pointed out when this sort of civics came to his local schools, it is "getting a bunch of teenagers out of chemistry class" to do "almost anything they wish as civic engagement."[121] Even a proponent of engagement, Peter Levine, acknowledged "that it often degenerates into apolitical and unintellectual service."[122]

At best, action civics is a watered down version of civic education and, arguably, does not provide much civic education at all. Taking field trips, doing community service projects, and engaging in student protests might seem like more fun than sitting in a classroom, but what are the students *learning*? It is capitulating

---

[121] Chester E. Finn Jr., "Civic engagement versus civics education," Thomas B. Fordham Institute, November 28, 2018, https://fordhaminstitute.org/national/commentary/civic-engagement-versus-civics-education.

[122] Peter Levine, "action civics goes mainstream and gets controversial," A Blog for Civic Renewal, January 23, 2012, https://peterlevine.ws/?p=7974.

to the difficulty of teaching history and civics in the classroom and doing something that students will enjoy more. No doubt there are diligent people who find lessons arising from action civics, but even then, we are putting the cart of civic engagement before the horse of civic education, with unfortunate consequences for the learning of civics and American history.

Action Civics as Politics by Another Name

Although proponents of action civics argue that it is apolitical and largely focused on nonpartisan local projects, that may not be its net effect. In order to most effectively engage students, action civics often calls on students to take action on projects they care about. Sometimes, these are nonpartisan local issues, such as the students in Anaheim, California, who researched water quality in their drinking fountains or the students in Chicago who sought to move a bus stop to a safer location.[123] But young people these days are often appealed to by activists for larger issues such as climate change and social justice, which tend to be more toward the liberal end of the political scale. One critic of action civics examined the projects on the Generation Citizen website and found "virtually all of them focused on priorities of the political left, such as the Green New Deal and gun control."[124] In a major

---

[123] Catherine Gewertz, "'Action Civics' Enlists Students in Hands-On Democracy," Education Week, March 20, 2019, https://www.edweek.org/policy-politics/action-civics-enlists-students-in-hands-on-democracy/2019/03.

[124] John Sailer, "Training students to protest doesn't a civics education make," Washington Times, July 6, 2021, https://www.washingtontimes.com/news/2021/jul/6/training-students-to-protest-doesnt-a-civics-educa/.

study of action civics, Thomas Lindsey found around half of the projects on Generation Citizen's website to be "disproportionately liberal and organized around protest."[125]

Perhaps action civics skewing left is an inevitable risk, but releasing thousands of young people into the political world to pursue their passions is not a responsible goal for civic education. If action civics continues to gain ground, it seems important for there to be a greater effort to balance projects politically or limit them to local or nonpartisan projects altogether. Perhaps the idea for a project could start from the passion of a student but be refined and revised through a deep study of our American history and principles. Otherwise, action civics will continue to open itself to deserved criticism for fanning political flames and not seeking greater civic knowledge and understanding. Of course, limiting projects to local questions, as proponents often claim, leaves students without exploring most of the questions now covered in civic education about the history and principles of the nation and their state.

Civic Action Should Follow Civic Knowledge: The Educational Problem

One major problem with action civics, then, is that it puts the cart of civic action and engagement ahead of the horse of civic knowledge—a flawed educational approach we would

[125] Thomas K. Lindsay and Lucy Vander Laan, "'Action Civics,' 'New Civics,' 'Civic Engagement,' and 'Project-Based Civics': Advances in Civic Education?," Texas Public Policy Foundation, September 1, 2020, https://www.texaspolicy.com/action-civicsnew-civics-civic-engagement-and-project-based-civics-advances-in-civic-education/.

not countenance in science or other fields of inquiry. In the scientific method, for example, students first learn in the classroom, then they form a hypothesis about how something works, only then going into the lab or out into the field to test their hypothesis. Then, they return to the classroom to write up their results and learn from their experimentation. Knowledge sandwiches the scientific experiment, coming both before and after the fieldwork. To do otherwise puts learning at risk in favor of ungrounded activism.

This pedagogical problem with action civics has been widely noted. Education expert Robert Pondiscio refers to it as "something of a civic education sugar rush" with the "momentary thrill of public engagement" without in-depth understanding.[126] Using another apt analogy, Pondiscio calls "operational citizenship" without an understanding of America's history and political principles, "a civic-education snake with its head cut off—a whole lot of action that lacks intentionality, context, and ultimately, meaning."[127]

Seth Andrew, who helped launch Democracy Prep in Harlem,[128] agrees that moving toward civic skills and action

---

[126] Robert Pondiscio, "Seizing the Moment to Improve Civics Education," Thomas B. Fordham Institute, November 29, 2017, https://fordhaminstitute.org/national/commentary/seizing-moment-improve-civics-education.

[127] Ibid.

[128] Unfortunately, Mr. Andrew has more recently been charged with misusing funds belonging to the charter schools he helped found. (See: Dan Mangan, "Former Obama education advisor Seth Andrew in talks to resolve charter school theft case," CNBC, May 28, 2023, https://www.cnbc.com/2021/05/28/former-obama-advisor-seth-andrew-in-talks-to-resolve-charter-school-theft.html.) Nevertheless, the approach of the schools on civic education seems worth noting.

without building a base of knowledge in history and government is the wrong approach. His teachers, he has said, "want kids to know stuff before they attempt to do stuff."[129] He argues that there needs to be a floor of historical and civic knowledge before moving on to other approaches. It is his view that without knowing how government works and its core principles, teaching civic skills will not create productively engaged citizens.

We need to think of the important questions students need to be able to address on any subject, including history and civics. Action civics addresses the "how" question, at least in the very limited case study in which a particular student may be engaged, but plenty of larger "how" questions, at the federal and state level for example, are not addressed. Students really need to know the "what" as well as the "how:" What are the fundamental principles of our republic, and what is behind them? The "why" questions—the deepest of all—are certainly neglected in an action civics format: Why was our republic formed as it was, why has it changed over time, and why does it need to be maintained or changed now? Those deeper questions, passionately debated throughout our history, are hardly rote or boring.

Action civics not only has a bias toward action over knowledge, but also a disposition in favor of change over continuity. Young people are challenged to go out and find something in the civic world that needs to be fixed or improved. They are not trying to understand the way things work, or should work, or to evaluate how things are working and why. It is not to respect a system that, despite challenges, may be functioning reasonably

---

[129] Holly Korbey, Building Better Citizens: A New Civics Education For All (Boulder, CO: Rowman & Littlefield, 2019), 37.

well. It is to seek not understanding but change, assuming that change is what every situation needs.

It would be more accurate to describe action civics as a course in political change rather than civic education. It is actually a tool designed to try to fix American democracy—at least as some people feel it should be fixed—rather than fix civic education itself in order to develop "informed patriots" with civic understanding. It should not be surprising, then, to learn that action civics now finds itself in a large political battle.

Action Civics as a Battleground: The Politicization Problem

Proponents of action civics who believe it is merely an extension of service learning or civic engagement are surprised that it has become a major political battleground. There are several reasons action civics is politically controversial. For one thing, because it diminishes civic knowledge in favor of action, it runs afoul of those who believe in primacy of studying the classics of American thought. To make matters worse, because the projects sometimes skew to the political left, action civics portends the unleashing of political protests and action by young people for school credit, "supposing dubiously," as scholar Peter Berkowitz points out, "that schools are well-suited to direct outside-the-classroom action."[130]

Conservatives, then, have risen up against action civics as a substitute for teaching civic knowledge. Stanley Kurtz, a scholar

---

[130] Peter Berkowitz, "The Civic-Education Battles," RealClearPolitics, May 30, 2021, https://www.realclearpolitics.com/articles/2021/05/30/the_civic-education_battles_145849.html.

with the Ethics and Public Policy Center, has led the conservative political charge against action civics. In a series of articles in *National Review* and elsewhere, Kurtz has laid out the conservative critique of action civics, its path toward fuller implementation, and he has actively fostered political action to block it.

Although action civics is used by schools and districts in a number of states, Kurtz points out that prior to 2021, only two states had mandated action civics: Illinois and Massachusetts. He argues that the action civics law in Illinois, passed in 2015, has taken on a very liberal political bent by 2021.[131] Kurtz points out that new "Culturally Responsive Teaching and Leading Standards" adopted in Illinois will combine with action civics to push large numbers of young people into left-leaning political protest and action.[132] In an article in the *Washington Examiner*, Kurtz describes Massachusetts as "ground zero" for academics and practitioners to use action civics in a major leftward assault on K–12 education.[133]

Now, in addition to presidential election battleground states, we have action civics battleground states. In Texas, for example, legislation has been considered that would ban the teaching of action civics.[134] Governor Ron DeSantis of Florida, an

---

[131] Stanley Kurtz, "Ultra-Woke Illinois Mandates Are Top Threat to U.S. Education," National Review, January 19, 2021, https://www.nationalreview.com/corner/ultra-woke-illinois-mandates-are-top-threat-to-u-s-education/.

[132] Ibid.

[133] Stanley Kurtz, "Democrats plot path to dominance," Washington Examiner, February 25, 2021, https://www.washingtonexaminer.com/politics/democrats-plot-path-to-dominance.

[134] Stanley Kurtz, "Knocks on Texas Civics Bill Ring Hollow," National Review, May 4, 2021, https://www.nationalreview.com/corner/knocks-on-texas-civics-bill-ring-hollow/.

active proponent of improving civic education, surprised many by vetoing a bill that included action civics.[135] Similarly, conservative South Dakota governor Kristi Noem has expressed her opposition to the teaching of action civics.[136] Action civics is also being considered and debated in Rhode Island, Oregon, New York, Georgia, and elsewhere. It has become at once the solution to our civic education problems for many and the destruction of true civic education for others.

Oklahoma provides an interesting case study. Establishing action civics in the state was an early project for Generation Citizen. In general, Oklahomans felt something was being done to advance civic education in their state. Later, however, especially as Texas and other states began to oppose action civics, Oklahomans wondered about the politics of the program. The Oklahoma Council of Public Affairs noted that Oklahoma legislators had banned the study of Critical Race Theory but also argued that the state legislature needed to ban action civics or their work would be "only half done."[137] The report went on to describe action civics as "Critical Race Theory in practice."

135 Danielle J. Brown, "DeSantis vetoes civic education bill citing 'action civics' — programs that critics call leftist," Florida Phoenix, June 30, 2021, https://floridaphoenix.com/2021/06/30/desantis-vetoes-civic-education-bill-citing-action-civics-programs-that-critics-call-leftist/

136 Cory Allen Heidelberger, "Noem Would Ban Real-World Civics Education, Reduce Teaching of Community Involvement to Theoretical Exercises," Dakota Free Press, January 11, 2022, https://dakotafreepress.com/2022/01/11/noem-would-ban-real-world-civics-education-reduce-teaching-of-community-involvement-to-theoretical-exercises/.

137 David Randall, "Oklahoma Lawmakers Should Ban Action Civics," Oklahoma Council of Public Affairs, August 4, 2021, https://www.ocpathink.org/post/oklahoma-lawmakers-should-ban-action-civics.

The Federal Role and Action Civics

Controversy about action civics has also arisen in connection with a bipartisan federal bill in support of civic education. The Civics Secures Democracy Act,[138] introduced by Senators Christopher Coons (D-DE) and John Cornyn (R-TX), seeks to provide a major $1 billion boost in federal spending on civic education. Although the bill was generally well received initially, it turns out that the devil is in the details, as the bill calls for particular types of civic education. It specifies aid not only to programs that develop civic knowledge—the term often used to describe traditional civic education—but also to programs developing civic skills, dispositions, and behaviors, which is more akin to action civics and other newer ideas. The bill becomes even more prescriptive, channeling grants to programs that pursue "evidence-based practices," including service learning, civics projects, and instruction on current issues and events. The bill addresses improving civic engagement as well as civic education.

This federal bill, and similar ones that have been introduced in recent years but ended up stalled in committees, is both promising and troublesome. It is promising in that the call we make for an "all-hands on deck" national effort toward civic education could, indeed, include the federal government. As noted previously, the federal government formerly provided financial support for civic education, peaking at around $150 million per year in fiscal year 2010. After this, Congress cut the funding, shifting money toward STEM

---

[138] Congress.gov, "Text - S.879 - 117th Congress (2021-2022): Civics Secures Democracy Act," March 22, 2021, https://www.congress.gov/bill/117th-congress/senate-bill/879/text.

education instead. As previously mentioned, one report pointed out that the federal government now spends around $5 million per year on civics, compared to almost $3 billion a year on STEM.[139] This adds up to $54 per schoolchild per year on STEM and a mere 5 cents per student on civics.[140]

One of the most troublesome aspects of federal investments in civic education is that there are federal strings attached to what ought to be a state and local matter. Prior to the No Child Left Behind legislation twenty years ago, K–12 education had long been the purview of state and local governments. Under No Child Left Behind, federal testing and reforms began to intrude heavily on the school day. Later, introduction of a Common Core curriculum also appeared to state and local governments to intrude on their territory. Finally, with sufficient pushback from teachers and parents, No Child Left Behind was not renewed and the Every Student Succeeds Act took its place in 2015, restoring power and initiative to the states for K–12 education. It is one of few cases where federal power was actually turned back to state and local governments.

Federal legislation, then, that puts out the carrot of a $1 billion investment in civic education but the stick of federal oversight and standards for the type of civic education it will support, moves in the wrong direction. As critics have pointed out, it also very much opens the door that the service learning and project aspects of the bill could lead to a kind of federal endorsement

---

[139] National Commission, Inspired to Serve, 15.

[140] Kimberly Adams, "What Federal Funding for Civics Reveals About American Political Discourse," Marketplace, November 6, 2019, https://www.marketplace.org/2019/11/06/what-federal-funding-for-civics-reveals-about-american-political-discourse/.

and funding of action civics specifically. In fact, one expert has noted that in a related Civic Learning Act of 2021, "half the priorities direct funding toward 'action civics.'"[141] Stanley Kurtz argues that these federal standards could lead to an effort to impose a national curriculum for civic education.[142] If the federal government is to support civic education at all, it would be far better that it return to the role it played a decade ago: providing support for teacher education in the content of American history and civics without federal curricular strings.

"Lived Civics" Seeking Its Place

Scholars have recently developed a new approach to civic education especially relevant to ethnic minority students called "lived civics." Lived civics suggests that instead of starting with history or government, civic education should begin with the experiences of students and their ethnic communities. A document titled *Let's Go There* lays out the lived civics premise and approach.[143] The argument is that, rather than adding ethnic citizenship experience on top of a traditional civics or history course, teachers need to begin with the students' own experiences and that of their ethnic communities, which includes community action through civil rights movements, campaigns against income inequality, and the like. Here, the priority is

---

[141] Sailer, "Training students to protest."

[142] Field, "Teaching 'action civics.'"

[143] Cathy Cohen et al., Let's Go There: Making a Case for Race, Ethnicity and a Lived Civics Approach to Civic Education, February 23, 2018, https://static1.squarespace.com/static/5e20c70a7802d9509b9aeff2/t/5e66cd4fe ddd0f57bb759f21/1583795568756/LetsGoThere_Paper_V17.pdf.

refocusing the lens through which civic education is viewed to feature ethnic experience and action.

Needless to say, lived civics has its critics.[144] For one thing, it reverses the teaching process to begin not with the teacher and the course material, but with the students' experiences. Then, too, lived civics prioritizes actions and experiences rather than serious historical and civic knowledge. Indeed, in some forms, it would deny that objective civic knowledge is truly possible. Lived civics is beginning to receive attention as a solution to problems of social justice and racism alleged to be in the standard curriculum. It seems to be the new, new version of action civics combined with Critical Race Theory.

If Better Civic Education Is the Question, Action Civics Is Not the Answer

It seems clear that the problems in civic education are not solved by having young people do community service and political projects. At best, action civics puts civic engagement ahead of civic knowledge. Worse, one can make the case that action civics is not really civic education at all; rather, it is a kind of political awareness and engagement that skims the surface of today's problems without going deeply into the foundations, purposes, and systems of our republic. Students are not prepared to address political or governmental issues of the day without understanding the system itself and how it has developed over time. Further, action civics has added more fuel to the already raging political

---

[144] See, for example, John D. Sailer, "Anti-civics," City Journal, July 16, 2021, https://www.city-journal.org/article/anti-civics.

fire that is spreading across our legislatures as well as our schools about the teaching of US history and civics. It is the wrong solution at the wrong time.

Although action civics should be discarded as a replacement for civic education and rejected as the new and better civics it is touted to be, it could play a secondary role. Properly designed and carried out, limited use of civic projects could be a helpful supplement to civic knowledge. Just as a science experiment provides hands-on experience to validate or reject a hypothesis, a properly done civic project in the curriculum could enhance student engagement and learning. But this requires a much deeper and more fully developed educational experience than merely sending students out into the world to connect with issues they may care about.

For example, there is evidence to support the idea that having students begin the voter registration process during school could be a useful civic project. Students would not only study the history and principles of republican government and the duty of citizens to vote but would also begin the process of registering to vote that would become effective later when they turn eighteen. This idea has gained some traction across the country with nearly half of states having implemented it in some form.[145] Research has shown that making voter registration part of the civics curriculum has the benefit of increasing young voter turnout, which has been an ongoing challenge.[146]

One could readily envision other projects that could supplement and enhance learning but not replace civic knowledge as the

---

[145] Sparks, "How States and Schools."

[146] John B. Holbein and D. Sunshine Hillygus, Making Young Voters: Converting Civic Attitudes Into Civic Action, 2010.

core priority. The key would be to offer a very limited number of nonpartisan projects that coordinate well with knowledge portions of the civics course. In this way, students would, in effect, carry out experiments that applied to and supplemented their classroom learning. If students are interested in current political reform, for example, a deeper study of the history of reform movements over time will greatly enhance their education and experience. As a modest supplement, civic projects would avoid the valid charge that action civics puts the cart of action ahead of the horse of knowledge and generates politicized outcomes.

Far from solving the problem of poor civic education in our schools, action civics basically moves the goalpost from learning to action. It redefines the purpose of civic education as getting students out of the classroom and involved in solving today's civic problems. Action civics is highly problematic educationally and threatens to add to the distracting and dangerous political wildfires already menacing the teaching of American history and civics.

CHAPTER FOUR

Discovering the "Why" of America: The Foundation of a Good Civic Education

Civic Education as Information

It's one thing to understand the problem of civic education; it's another to address the problem. How do we fix the problem? When a house is falling down, you need to shore up the foundation and perhaps even rebuild it. To rebuild civic education, we must do the same thing: restore a solid understanding of the philosophy of civic education on which to build our house. That strong foundation starts with sound principles of education. In this chapter, we will present the foundation—the philosophy—on which we will build our recommendations for a revitalized education in American history and civics.

To build a solid foundation for civic education, we must start with the right understanding of education itself. Unfortunately, there are many wrong or incomplete understandings of education that shape the way we teach civic education. We have already seen in the discussions of action civics and the 1619 Project that civic education must not be a form of indoctrination whose predetermined purpose is to "change the system," whether that change is produced directly by action (action civics) or by criticism that necessarily leads to action to change the system (the 1619 Project). Civic education as action presupposes (and imposes) predetermined actions or outcomes on students who do not have the knowledge necessary to evaluate the rightness of those actions and outcomes. The proper goal of civic education is not civic action or political criticism; it is informed citizenship. Out of such citizenship necessarily comes civic action and criticism, but those are the effect of civic education, not the cause. As informed citizens, students must have a solid foundation of knowledge from which they engage public issues.

In rejecting civic education as action, however, we should not think of civic education as the student passively receiving information. Unfortunately, this is still the dominant idea in the American educational system. While there is some dispute among historians, education reformers such as Frederick Hess argue that this understanding of education as "transmission of information to the student" owes much to ideas adapted from the large-scale industrial mode of production in the late nineteenth and early twentieth centuries.[147] Even if mass industry was not the education reformers' explicit model, it is still true

---

[147] Rick Hess, "There's Nothing Especially Educational About Factory-Style Management," Education Week, April 9, 2014, www.edweek.org/education/opinion-theres-nothing-especially-educational-about-factory-style-management/2014/04.

that much of K–12 education developed "factory-like" elements.[148] For example, for the sake of efficiency, the scientific discovery of knowledge is transformed into consumable information by mass production systems. In civic education, it is made up of experts in colleges of education who "train" teachers; division of subjects into distinct categories such as "American history" and "American government"; teachers who specialize in those distinct categories; and even schools organized like factories with assembly lines—such as a bell ringing to tell students when to move from the classroom of a teacher who specializes in the transmission of information of one subject ("American history") to another teacher who specializes in the transmission of information of another ("civics").[149] The information produced is to be consumed by the student, who memorizes it and then regurgitates it on a test.

In this situation, the textbook inevitably becomes powerful. While the teacher is understood primarily as a transmitter of information to the students, teachers cannot know and transmit enough information on their own because—as teachers will readily say—they have not always received the education they need, which too often focuses on pedagogy, not content. So both the students and the teacher need a textbook, whose creation is

---

148 Valerie Strauss, "American schools are modeled after factories and treat students like widgets. Right? Wrong.," Washington Post, October 10, 2015, https://www.washingtonpost.com/news/answer-sheet/wp/2015/10/10/american-schools-are-modeled-after-factories-and-treat-students-like-widgets-right-wrong/.

149 Bernie Bleske, "The Myth of So-Called 'Factory Education,'" Medium, March 8, 2019, https://medium.com/s/story/are-schools-really-factories-ed539f6b2ebe.

supervised (or advised) by an expert or group of experts.[150] The textbook is supposed to be designed according to the age or cognitive development of the student so as to present the collected information in as easily "ingestible" a form as possible, in an organized and abbreviated form.[151]

While knowing important facts is an essential part of sound civic education, forcing teachers to operate on the idea of "education as information" and a concomitant reliance on textbooks has had a harmful effect on American history and civics education. As we have already seen, civic education has increasingly become a matter of political dispute, which means that one of the most important and potentially divisive decisions faced by a social studies department, school, school district, or state is the choice of a textbook. As a result, a school's history and civics curriculum either becomes immediately politicized or ineffective as people choose a textbook that is as inoffensive as possible.

Another negative result is that the teacher's role as the primary educator is devalued or at least made more difficult. Because textbooks are supposed to hold the information that constitutes "education," the teacher's job becomes to "present" the information in the textbook. Teachers are induced, or even forced, to become reliant on the textbook. At some point, the

---

[150] Don Waters, "Who Gets To Write Public-School History Textbooks?," Slate Magazine, October 22, 2010, https://slate.com/news-and-politics/2010/10/who-gets-to-write-public-school-history-textbooks.html.

[151] "Review of Graph Comprehension Research: Implications for Instruction," March 2002, Educational Psychology Review 14(1).

textbook becomes the teacher.[152] Many teachers—especially those who love to educate young people—try to resist by supplementing the textbook with their own materials or insights. Yet the textbook—if it is used—necessarily sets the tone for the student's experience of American history and government and too often becomes the educational framework for the classroom.

The third and most serious problem with "education as information" is that American history and civics become so boring that teachers do not have the opportunity to cultivate the kind of engaged citizens needed for our republic. History and civics become largely a matter of memorizing discrete and often disconnected facts or theories—the "what" of America. Research has shown, however, that while "many learners find it difficult to remember facts related to historical events or figures…the fluid narrative of storytelling can tie facts together into a more meaningful pattern."[153]

This is because learning by stories is a way to understand the "why" of facts by placing them in a meaningful context. As Aristotle said long ago, human beings, by nature, desire to know "why"—to understand the purposes and principles of things, an interest that grows stronger as the mind matures.[154] The human mind grows in middle and high school students in

---

[152] André Simu, The Textbook – Servant or Master?: A Study of the Role of Textbooks in English Second Language Learning in Swedish High Schools, 2019, http://www.diva-portal.org/smash/get/diva2:1281651/FULLTEXT01.pdf.

[153] NMAH, "Teaching history by telling stories," National Museum of American History, November 4, 2010, https://americanhistory.si.edu/blog/2010/11/teaching-history-by-telling-stories.html.

[154] Aristotle, Metaphysics, Book A, section 1.

such a way that students become more interested in the "why" rather than just the "what" or "how."

This was the insight behind the classical taxonomy of education into grammar, logic, and rhetoric. As educator Susan Wise Bauer notes, the "grammar" phase was for younger children (grades K–5) who are excited to learn facts about the world, especially through stories. As children grow older and their intellectual capacity expands (grades 6–8), they enter the "logic" phase in which they are not satisfied to understand the "what" but also need to understand the "why" more directly through "logic." At this stage, they try to understand "why" by "pulling things apart" through argumentation. The "rhetoric" phase is for the oldest children (grades 9–12) whose capacity has expanded such that they understand "why" by pulling things apart and then putting things back together through synthesizing.[155] Given these stages of adolescent development, just memorizing facts does not satisfy the intellectual needs of adolescents, which means that they will not be intellectually engaged or excited by history and civics classrooms based on simply transmitting and memorizing information. They may ingest the information out of necessity ("I have to pass the class"), fear ("I don't want a bad grade"), internal discipline ("I'm a hard worker"), and/or pre-existing interest ("I've always liked history"), but it will not be the kind of experience that cultivates an interest in or love for American history and government, and it will not become a part of their minds and hearts as citizens.

Learning facts by themselves—for example, about how government works—is of limited usefulness in forming citizens if it

---

[155] Susan Wise Bauer, "What Is Classical Education?," Well Trained Mind Press, June 3, 2009, https://welltrainedmind.com/a/classical-education/.

is disconnected from the "why" of America. As teachers know, they cannot simply tell a middle or high school student that it is important to understand how government works. A student will not truly care if he or she doesn't know why it is important to understand that fact. And the only way to understand the "why" is to dig into the bigger and deeper questions that give meaning to the "how." Why do we have a republic? Why a constitution? Why are there three branches of government? Why do we have freedom of speech or religion? The purposes of a country determine "how" its government works and shape the character of its people. As Americans such as Thomas Jefferson, Abraham Lincoln, and Martin Luther King Jr. have reminded us at critical moments in our history, understanding the "why" of America is the key to understanding what it means to be an American. It is perhaps not a surprise, then, that national tests show students performing so poorly on American history and civics. Too little time is spent on history and civics, and when those areas are covered, the system too often forces teachers to teach by rote. This is hardly the recipe for an engaging or formative experience.

Civic Education as Critical Thinking Skills

Another dominant understanding is to think of education as the development of critical thinking skills. This view of education can be traced to the early twentieth-century reaction against the information-based industrial model of education. Early versions of the critical thinking model were championed in America by progressive educational theorists such as John

Dewey, who introduced the term "critical thinking" as the goal of education.[156] For Dewey, the emerging fields of modern natural science and sociology provide decisive insights for K–12 education. Modern natural science (such as Heisenberg's Uncertainty Principle) shows that facts do not simply "exist": they are created as "facts" by the interpretations human beings give to phenomena they encounter.[157] From modern sociology, Dewey concluded that interpretations of phenomena are created by the social organizations within which people live. Society supplies the values through which people interpret the world. Building on these insights from emerging twentieth-century academic disciplines, Dewey argued that the mind is satisfied not by taking in preexisting "facts," but by creatively producing ideas about the various possibilities of a fact or argument.[158] In Dewey's view, "how to think" is a skill that needs to be developed and is in fact the most important mental and spiritual disposition. Social progress is advanced by understanding how social organization produced a fact or argument and how the fact or argument can be used to advance such progress. In developing critical thinking skills, the argument goes: it is much less important what students learn and much more about developing the

---

[156] David Hitchcock, "Critical Thinking," The Stanford Encyclopedia of Philosophy (Winter 2022 Edition), eds. Edward N. Zalta and Uri Nodelman, https://plato.stanford.edu/entries/critical-thinking/history.html.

[157] Joaquín Fernández Mateo, "John Dewey's theory of inquiry. Quantum physics, ecology and the myth of the scientific method," December 2020, Agora papeles de Filosofía 40(1):133–154.

[158] John Dewey, The School and Society, 1900; in Journal of Educational Sciences and Psychology, vol. VI (LXVIII), no. 1B/2016, 66–70, "John Dewey's contributions in the field of Sociology of Education," Ana-Maria Aurelia Petrescua.

skill of how to think about information and arguments. If *Tyler Makes Pancakes!* gets students to think, it is not any less valuable than the Gettysburg Address.

While critical thinking is an essential part of civic education, it is not enough by itself. Just as "education as information" is fundamentally about the "what," "education as critical thinking skills" is essentially about the "how." Unfortunately, as E. D. Hirsch says, research has shown that students cannot think critically in the abstract: they must think critically *about something*, which means that they must know important facts about the subject they are going to think about.[159] For example, a student cannot think critically about the constitutionality of President Lincoln's suspension of habeas corpus during the Civil War unless she knows some important facts from the Constitution, especially Articles I and II. Most importantly, learning how to think about an issue in American history and government does not tell a student what issue is worth thinking about—why it is important to them as an American. In other words, learning "how" does not mean learning the "why" of America, which means that critical thinking cannot answer the basic question: Why should I learn this?

---

[159] E. D. Hirsch, The Schools We Need: And Why We Don't Have Them (1999).

Civic Education as Discovering the "Why" of America

The Human Mind Is Free: A Pedagogy of Questions

What we need, then, is a civic education with a foundation that combines the "what" and "how" in such a way that the students learn the "why" of America. Such civic education must be based on two fundamental truths or axioms. The first is that, as Thomas Jefferson put it in the Virginia Statute of Religious Freedom, "Almighty God hath created the mind free." The human mind is free to rise above the accidents of time, place, class, race, and gender to pursue the truth. Of course, there is no such thing as an "objective" person who has no preexisting opinions, including opinions on America. All students and teachers come to the classroom with their own particular perspectives. But real civic education rests on the truth that minds with preexisting opinions can meet across time and place to learn from each other. A white woman in the twenty-first century, for example, can learn important insights about what it means to be truly free from a nineteenth-century black man like Frederick Douglass. Or as W. E. B. Du Bois put it in *The Souls of Black Folk*:

> I sit with Shakespeare, and he winces not. Across the color line I move arm and arm with Balzac and Dumas, where smiling men and welcoming women glide in gilded halls. From out of the caves of evening that swing between the strong-limbed Earth and the tracery of stars, I summon Aristotle and Aurelius and what soul I will, and they come all graciously with no

scorn nor condescension. So, wed with Truth, I
dwell above the veil.

This means that education—including civic education—is not
about indoctrination, information, or learning how to think,
but about discovering the truth for oneself. Discovering the
truth requires knowing facts and how to think about them, but
it also—and primarily—means grasping the "why" of something. In the case of civic education, it is discovering the "why"
of America: the principles and purposes of our country.

Someone might object that the idea of America having a
"why" assumes that America is a coherent whole with a moral
purpose, or telos as Aristotle would have called it. Contemporary
civic education assumes more and more that while America may
be a geographic entity, it is not a coherent moral one—it has
many "stories" that share nothing essential in common. Or,
if there is a commonality among the stories, it is the story of
inequality of power among groups and injustice done by the
dominant group to others. We believe, however, that the proper
foundation for civic education is the idea that America has a
moral essence derived from the principles of the Declaration of
Independence and the Constitution, that America's purpose is
to fulfill those principles, and that our history is the story of our
struggle to fulfill them.

Civic education as the "discovery of America's purpose" necessarily implies a certain way of teaching and learning (a "pedagogy"). American history and government should be framed by
questions, not by facts or predetermined lenses. For example, an
assignment should not be "Name the most important parts of
FDR's New Deal" but "Why did FDR think that the New Deal
was good for America? Was he right?" To answer that question, a

student must know the important facts (the "what") of the Great Depression and New Deal, but she must know more than that. She also must understand FDR's arguments and the powers of the federal government under the Constitution. She must even make a judgment about whether FDR was right. Making such a judgment requires the cultivation of critical thinking skills (the "how"), but such critical thinking must be rooted in facts and directed toward answering the important "why" question. Moreover, making such a judgment requires having an opinion about what is right for America. To do that, the student must have some opinion or knowledge of what America means, including the American Founding.

This sequence leads back to the ultimate framing question of a good civic education: What does it mean to be an American? An American is not just a citizen but a kind of human being—a self-governing human being. It is a person whose mind and heart are profoundly shaped by the principles articulated in the Declaration of Independence and illuminated in the history of America, and who has the knowledge, virtues, and judgment necessary to govern himself as an individual and as part of a family, community, and nation. Starting from the question of what it means to be an American distinguishes true civic education from other theories that start by dividing students into crude categories (for example, being a white American means being privileged; being a black American means being a victim of oppression). Instead, we must start from a unifying question that applies to all students and provides a common ground for thinking. Asking the question "What does it mean to be an American?" will elicit many diverse answers—at least at first, because students come from many different backgrounds and experiences. This means that there is not an immediate answer that is obvious to the student. It must be found, which requires knowing historical facts, understanding fundamental principles, and thinking through the meaning of those principles. Again, this approach does not preclude or ignore disagreement and dissent. Instead, it welcomes those as part of the ongoing struggle over the meaning and application of our principles.

It is vital to understand, however, that answering the question of what it means to be an American cannot be done in the abstract. An "American" is not an idea; as we said, it is a kind of human being, and people live in time and space with distinct and shared experiences. So the question must be studied historically—as part of the American story. Students must discover the particular experiences and arguments that produced who we are as Americans. For example, why did Americans at the time of the Founding believe that Congress—not the president—should have the power to declare war? And why has Congress used that power so rarely over the course of American history, despite the country's many military conflicts? Does it mean that Americans are a militaristic people who don't care about the legal niceties of war? Or are they reluctant to enter war and therefore have an aversion to declaring it? Does it depend on the era? These questions must be studied by looking at the time of the Founding as well as subsequent American history such as the Spanish-American War, World War II, and the Korean War. This means that a good civic education cannot be limited to "civics." It must combine the study of American history and government: history should be studied with a view toward understanding ourselves as Americans, and government should be studied as part of the American story. Only then can we understand both the moral essence of America—our founding principles—and our purpose in struggling to fulfill those principles.

In fact, a good civic education recognizes that history and government are not truly separate subjects. They both serve the same purpose—forming good Americans—and both study the same subject matter: the story of America. Politics and government profoundly shape history; much of history is political history. The principles of a country—above all, its view of justice—shape all of society and its way of life. They tell us how we should live (for example, everyone should be treated equally by the law) and provide a basis for criticizing society when it doesn't live that way (such as Martin Luther King Jr.'s nonviolent protests). America's founding political and moral principles have profoundly shaped our history and who we are as Americans. Conversely, the principles of government are not just abstract philosophical ideas; they are acted upon (or not) by people who exist in a particular time and place. So history and government are really two sides of the same civic education coin: government happens in history, and history is shaped by the principles of a country's government.

In building this foundation that combines history and government to understand the "why" of America, it is important to remember that we cannot try to force doctrines or conclusions onto students. We can't just declare to teenagers, "This is the purpose of America! Believe it!" Indoctrination is the opposite of respecting the freedom of the human mind, and it does not cultivate the habits of freedom. It's also boring, because it does not allow the excitement and pleasure of discovery. Young people need civic education organized around the principle that they have the opportunity to discover the truth about themselves as Americans and be part of the American story.

America Is Free: The Framework for the Questions

The good news is that some people have recognized the need for framing civic education around important questions—making it "inquiry-based," as practitioners like to say. For example, the Educating for American Democracy Roadmap calls itself "an inquiry-based content framework for excellence in civic and history education for all learners that is organized by major themes and questions, supported by key concepts."[160] But as a number of critics (and even friends) have pointed out, the EAD Roadmap lacks an explicit, guiding understanding of America that can direct its implementation.[161] While EAD aims to cultivate "honest patriotism" that "admits failures and celebrates praise," it tries not to take a position on the question of whether America should be defined by its successes or failures. This is not surprising given that the Roadmap was the product of over three hundred scholars, teachers, and practitioners from a wide variety of perspectives and produced in a very charged social and political environment. But civic education must have a clear position on this question because it is concerned with forming citizens who, as such, must have an opinion about whether and why their country deserves their attachment. So a good civic education must have a moral starting point on America that organizes the other questions framing the education.

---

[160] "We have created a roadmap," Educating for American Democracy.

[161] Rick Hess, "Civics Roadmap's Designers Would Do Well to Heed Their Critics," Education Week, April 12, 2021, https://www.edweek.org/teaching-learning/opinion-civics-roadmaps-designers-would-do-well-to-heed-their-critics/2021/04.

This brings us to the second foundational truth for reviving civic education: not only is the human mind free, but so is America. By this, we mean that America was founded on principles of self-government. These principles developed during the colonial period but were given their full definition and articulation in the Declaration of Independence, which—as Thomas Jefferson said—was meant to be "an expression of the American mind." These are the "self-evident" truths—the truths that are obvious once we have been enlightened to them—that united those Americans who favored independence: our principles come from the "laws of nature and of nature's God;" "all men are created equal;" all human beings have certain unalienable rights; it is government's job to "secure" equally through the rule of law; government must get its "just power" to secure our liberties from the "consent of the governed;" and the people always retain the right to change or abolish a government that is not doing its job or no longer has their consent. These are the principles of self-government proclaimed in the Declaration and embodied in state constitutions of the time and in the US Constitution. As a set, they serve as an indispensable part of the foundation of a good civic education, and it is essential that students study them.

"America is free" also means that our history is the story of our struggle to live up to our founding principles of freedom. It is one thing to be founded on principles of self-government; it is another thing to practice them. We know that America has fallen short—sometimes terribly, profoundly short—of practicing its principles. Consider the monstrous injustice of slavery or terrible treatment of Native Americans. Understanding the full meaning of the principles and putting them at the center of our public life has been a struggle for America. It is a story of discussion, debate, conflict, failure, and success in living out those principles. Fortunately, though, the story has a basic narrative arc that can make sense of the enormous number of discussions and debates: during the Founding, the American experiment in self-government was born; that experiment fell into crisis in the nineteenth century, especially in the fight over slavery that culminated in the Civil War; the meaning of the experiment was again debated in the late nineteenth and early twentieth centuries in the Progressive movement and the New Deal; and the Civil Rights Movement represented an attempt to bring those principles from the experiment to their fulfillment—to "live out the dream," as Martin Luther King Jr. put it. Understanding American history as a struggle over the meaning and practice of self-government allows civic education to do full justice to the failures and sins of America without giving into despair or teaching students that their country is irredeemably corrupt and can only be saved by being fundamentally transformed. It helps students discover a true story to be proud of, one in which they can see themselves being included no matter their background. Again, though, we must add this reminder: students cannot be forced to accept that "America is free"—they must be allowed to come to this conclusion for themselves, not be indoctrinated in it. That's the only way to respect the fact that the human mind is free and needs to discover the truth for itself.

Primary Sources and the Layer Cake of Civic Education

So far, this discussion of a philosophy or foundation for good civic education has been pretty abstract. It's one thing to know that we need to build civic education on the two principles that "the mind is free" and "America is free." It's another thing to actually put them together into something that works. How do we do that?

We have to build it layer by layer, as you would build a cake. The "cake" itself is the answer to the question: What does it mean to be an American? The principles that should frame civic education ("the mind is free," "America is free") are the recipe for making the cake. American history and government are two of the main ingredients that we use to make the cake, along with other subjects like geography and economics.

The ingredients are especially important. You can't make a great cake with bad flour or sugar. Likewise, you can't make great civic education without good historical and civic ingredients. Unfortunately, as we have seen, most civic education today uses a textbook as the main ingredient, which makes American history and civics either bland or unhealthy (or both).

Instead, we need to root all of our civic education in conversations based on primary sources. Lectures just transmit information; conversation awakens the mind to actually think about what it means to be an American. Thinking is not easy, especially for students used to just writing down and memorizing information, but it is exhilarating and enlivening. Once students get used to it, they cannot go back. By introducing the subject matter and spurring discussion through questions, the teacher supplies the ingredients, and through discovery by stories and conversation, the students put the ingredients together and bake the cake.

The conversations themselves need to be rooted in primary sources—documents like the Declaration of Independence, the Constitution, Lincoln's Gettysburg Address, and King's "I Have a Dream" speech and also letters, newspaper articles, political cartoons, laws, art, and music. All of these primary historical documents tell the story of America by those who lived and wrote it. Of course, not all who lived in the American story—for example, nineteenth-century African Americans—wrote about it or have been adequately represented in our primary documents. But more and more work is being done to incorporate those views and documents—for example, in voluminous slave narratives that have been published in recent years. Beyond historically marginalized communities, we have an amazing quality and variety of primary sources, starting with the Founding documents themselves.

Primary sources taste great (once students get used to them) and are good for students. They allow us to escape reliance on textbooks, which—as we have seen—are too often boring, biased, or both. For example, if we were going to determine if the original Constitution was a pro-slavery document (and therefore whether America was stained by slavery from the beginning), we would need to read and discuss the Constitution itself, along with the debates in the Constitutional Convention and the writings of *The Federalist*. Discussions based on primary sources are more interesting than lectures based on textbooks, because they recognize the depth and complexity of the issues at stake.

Primary sources also allow us to develop historical empathy by escaping "presentism": the impulse to view the past through the lens of the present and to judge the past according to contemporary standards. Using primary sources forces us to leave behind our own time and enter the past, which allows us to see that other people thought differently from us (and perhaps better). This challenges us to confront our own ideas of what it means to be an American. Before we can learn from history, we must understand people in the past as they understood themselves. Most importantly, entering the past immerses us in the story of America by having us directly encounter those who have come before. That immersion makes us feel part of the story, making it ours too. By bringing the past alive, primary sources make civic education more interesting, more complex, and more meaningful.

Primary sources have to be used wisely, however. First-graders cannot do a close, line-by-line reading of the Declaration of Independence. Like a good cake, civic education needs to be created layer by layer. The first layer is baked in elementary school. In grades K–5, children should approach civic education concretely through learning important facts (the "what") of our history and government. They should learn those facts primarily through stories. Children love stories: they love to hear them, they love to read them, and they love to write them. Children should learn the great stories of America, important facts, and a moral lesson derived from each story to help them understand what it means for them to be an American. The stories can have villains (as all good stories do), but they should focus on the heroes and how we can all be like them. The heroes would be people who advanced the principles of self-government through their own lives; the villains would be those who denied or tried to stop them. The stories should use pieces of primary documents so that students can hear the heroes in their own voice, but the primary documents are part of the larger story, not the story itself.

In middle school, we add another layer of complexity. Students start reasoning about the story of America they have learned. They study the course of American history from the beginning, this time rooted in primary documents. Using these documents, they question the facts and get below the surface, arguing over the meaning of these principles. They can now come to see that American history and government have often been a matter of discussion and dispute in which the "good guys" may have some flaws and the "bad guys" are rarely all bad. At this stage, primary documents become the basis of the conversation. They supply the arguments on both sides of an issue. For example, should America declare independence? Did the Founders support slavery? Should America become an imperial power?

In high school, the final layer of the cake is added. Students revisit primary documents from middle school on a deeper level and encounter new documents that add to the story. They now look to synthesize what they have learned and to understand how it all fits together in a coherent (if messy) story of America. They begin to understand the connections, for example, between the Declaration of Independence's proclamation of the principles of self-government, the Gettysburg Address's rearticulation of those principles to give America a "new birth of freedom" during and after the Civil War, and the "I Have a Dream" speech's call for America to finally live up to those principles in its law and society. They see the twentieth-century debate over the New Deal in light of the principles of the Declaration and Constitution—for example, do they mean the same thing as they did in the Founding, or should they be understood in a different way in new historical circumstances? They also come to see how America's principles have affected the debates over American foreign policy—for example, should America guide its foreign policy by promoting freedom around the world? In this final layer of the civic education cake, students see fully that America's principles are not just museum artifacts or philosophical abstractions, but they are at the heart of the events and debates that have animated the story of our history since the Founding.

As we've discovered at the Ashbrook Center, a multilayered civic education rooted in conversations based on primary sources has a powerful effect on students. It transforms them from passive recipients of information whose purpose they don't fully understand to active participants in discovering the American story and their place in it. Teachers who have learned this way of teaching and learning report that their classrooms are transformed into places where history and government come alive. They are places of real conversation about questions that matter to students. Because they learn why the historical facts matter, they actually retain the facts better. Studies show that AP US History scores of students in these kinds of classrooms increased 10 percent. Because the conversations are rooted in primary documents and not contemporary opinions, they can remain civil and even friendly on very sensitive issues. For example, by understanding Lincoln's view of the Founders' hopes for eventually eradicating slavery, students come to see that America was founded on principles of freedom, not oppression, and that those principles were only imperfectly realized during our Founding. They come to see that even though imperfect, America is—as Bill McClay says—truly "a land of hope" for everyone of all backgrounds.[162] This discovery inspires a love of country in students that is realistic and grounded in facts, and they ultimately understand why America deserves their love. It creates an "informed patriotism," as Ronald Reagan called it— the kind that lasts.

As we will see in the next chapter, the key to putting this civic education in place is educating teachers to spark conversation based on primary sources. Teachers are the most important determinant of what and how well students learn, and it is on them that the renewal of civic education will ultimately rest.

---

[162] McClay, Land of Hope: An Invitation to the Great American Story (2020).

CHAPTER FIVE

A Republic, If You Can Teach It

The Importance of Teachers

There are three legs to the K–12 civic education stool: state standards, curriculum, and teacher education. All three must be strong to bear the weight of educating the next generation of Americans. But if we are going to rebuild America's civic education, we must start with teachers. Because of their importance, they are the key: we must reach the young through those who teach the young.

We know what makes great teachers: they know their subject, love their subject, and love talking about it with students. Such teachers can have a profound effect on students. Who was your favorite teacher in school? What do you remember about him or her? Chances are you recall the effect they had on you—how they made you interested in a subject you never liked before; how they helped you discover a new idea or have a new thought; how, in some cases, they changed your life.

If you had a great history teacher, they made history come alive. They brought you back into the past and introduced you to fascinating people and important events. They showed you why history matters for today. If you had a great civics or government teacher, you learned what America's principles and form of government are and why they are worth understanding and respecting, even when they have not been fully followed. You learned something of what it means to be an American.

That's not surprising. Studies confirm what we know from our own experience: the quality of the teacher in the classroom is the most important factor in determining how well students learn.[163] It's not the facilities, the administrators, the state standards, or even the curriculum. All of those are factors, but in the end, as a RAND Corporation study puts it, "among school-related factors, teachers matter most... [T]eachers are estimated to have two to three times the effect of any other school factor, including services, facilities, and even leadership."[164] Teachers spend many hours in the classroom with our children; of course they are going to have a big effect on them. The only question is whether it will be negative or positive.

And the impact of teachers is more than just qualitative. One middle or high school educator can teach 125 students or

---

[163] Isaac M. Opper, "Teachers Matter," RAND Corporation, https://www.rand.org/education-and-labor/projects/measuring-teacher-effectiveness/teachers-matter.html.

[164] Ibid.

more in a year.[165] While the average teacher has about fourteen years of experience, a teacher can easily have a thirty-year or even forty-year career.[166] So, one teacher can educate up to 5,000 students—a huge multiplier effect.

Teachers can also influence other teachers, introducing their colleagues to their approach to teaching, and then those teachers reach their own students with that approach. Such a teacher can also inspire his or her students to become teachers, who then can reach their own 5,000 students. If, over the course of his career, a teacher inspires *only one* student to follow his example and converts *only one* colleague to his approach, that teacher still will have directly or indirectly affected the education of up to 15,000 students. Teachers are the key.

We especially need to focus on K–12 teachers, because for most Americans, high school (or sometimes even middle school) is the last opportunity to spend any serious time studying the history and principles of our country. In a survey of over one thousand US colleges and universities, the American Council of Trustees and Alumni found that less than 20 percent require a course in American history or government.[167] Many of those requirements can be filled by courses that do not focus on the

---

[165] "Average Public School Student: Teacher Ratio," Public School Review, https://www.publicschoolreview.com/average-student-teacher-ratio-stats/national-data.

[166] Madeline Will, "5 Things to Know About Today's Teaching Force," Education Week, October 23, 2018, https://www.edweek.org/leadership/5-things-to-know-about-todays-teaching-force/2018/10.

[167] American Council of Trustees and Alumni (ACTA), "What Will They Learn? 2021–2022: A Survey of Core Requirements at Our Nation's Colleges and Universities," https://www.goacta.org/ resource/what-will-they-learn-2021-2022/.

fundamental texts, principles, people, and events of America. So, the vast majority of American college students—who are already of voting age—are getting almost no real civic education from their university. That leaves high school and middle school as the last chance, and that leaves middle and high school teachers as the last chance of the last chance.

Unfortunately, a deep problem in civic education today is that too many K–12 teachers—including middle and high school history and government teachers—have not had the opportunity to become deeply knowledgeable in American history and civics. Many new teachers can relate to the challenge of staying just a few pages ahead of their students in the textbook, especially in those difficult first few years of teaching. Teachers who have not had the chance to become well versed in their subject will be unable to teach it to students; in fact, teachers often avoid topics they do not know well. The National Board for Professional Teaching Standards includes knowledge of content as one of its five core propositions for what teachers should know and be able to do: "Teachers know the subjects they teach and how to teach those subjects to students."[168] This is certainly true in American history and civics. As experts Diana Hess and John Zola pointed out, "The most transformative civic-learning programs are teacher-driven and teacher-dependent, as 'models of wisdom' and descriptions of high quality civic education demonstrate. The quality of teaching is the most

---

[168] Dat Le, "Teachers know the subjects they teach and how to teach those subjects to students," National Board for Professional Teaching Standards, December 21, 2016, https://www.nbpts.org/teachers-know-the-subjects-they-teach-and-how-to-teach-those-subjects-to-students/.

powerful determinant of students' access to a meaningful civic education."[169] Just as you cannot imagine teachers who are not computer literate leading a charge in computer literacy, we will not successfully transform student performance in civic education without teachers who are steeped in the material themselves and prepared to teach it effectively.

The Teacher Preparation Problem

Unfortunately, there are too many history and civics classrooms in America that are not having the profound effect they need to have. Students often report that they are bored and detached in history class.[170] This is not the fault of teachers, however. It is the fault of the kind of education they have received and a misunderstanding by those who educate teachers about what teachers are supposed to do in the classroom. As notable education scholar Diane Ravitch says, "[t]he greatest need in history education today is for well-prepared teachers who have studied history and who know how to make it vivid for youngsters."[171] Of course, not everyone has the ability to make history "vivid" by asking great questions or inspiring young hearts and minds—just

---

[169] Diana Hess and John Zola, "Professional Development as a Tool for Improving Civic Education," in David E. Campbell, Meira Levinson, Frederick M. Hess (eds), Making Civics Count: Citizenship Education for a new Generation (Cambridge: Harvard Education Press, 2012), 184.

[170] Valerie Strauss, "Why so many students hate history — and what to do about it," Washington Post, May 17, 2017, https://www.washingtonpost.com/news/answer-sheet/wp/2017/05/17/why-so-many-students-hate-history-and-what-to-do-about-it/.

[171] Diane Ravitch, "Coaches Shouldn't Teach History," History News Network, April 10, 2003, https://historynewsnetwork.org/article/1417.

as not everyone has the ability to be a professional dancer or comedian. There is a baseline of talent required for teaching, just as with any other profession. Other instructors might have the talent, but they are disposed simply to "get through the material" by making students take notes on information presented because it is easier than serious reading of a primary document. Unfortunately, as Professor Theodore Christou of Queen's University argues, "When students are taking notes in the history and social studies classroom, they are not learning history. They are learning how to take notes."[172]

There are, of course, many people who have the talent and disposition to be great history and civics teachers, but they have not had the opportunity to get the education they need. As Ravitch noted above, we must have "well-prepared teachers." Most middle and high school teachers are educated in schools or colleges of education at universities.[173] Unfortunately, too much of current teacher education in history and civics is not education at all, but training focused on the skills of pedagogy (how to teach) rather than content mastery (what to teach). As Ravitch says, "the majority of those who teach history in our schools are teaching out of their field. According to data from the US Department of Education, a majority of history teachers in grades 7–12 lack either a college major or minor or graduate degree in history. In many cases, they majored in education, not

---

[172] Dr. Theodore Christou, "Does History Have To Be Boring?," imaginED, May 31, 2016, https://www.educationthatinspires.ca/2016/05/31/does-history-have-to-be-boring/.

[173] Jenny DeMonte, "Who Is In Charge of Teacher Preparation?," Center for American Progress, June 17, 2013, https://www.americanprogress.org/article/who-is-in-charge-of-teacher-preparation/

in an academic subject. The only field that has more out-of-field teaching than history is the physical sciences, that is, physics and chemistry."[174]

College students intending to become teachers are generally not required to undertake majors in fields in which they will teach, and since many don't declare majors until the beginning of their junior year in college, they may not even know then that they will pursue a career in teaching. The problem is exacerbated in civic education because that is not generally available as a major. Civic education is a combination of history, government, geography, and economics—all the things required for good citizenship—and rarely could a student design a major covering all those fields.

Not surprisingly, then, a study, published in 2015 by the National Center for Education Statistics, showed that 78 percent of high school civics and government courses are taught by teachers who neither majored in those fields in college nor are certified to teach those specialties.[175] Only 6.8 percent of civics and government teachers surveyed had majored in those fields, with only 7.1 percent of these classes taught by majors[176]— numbers much lower than those found for other high school

---

[174] Ravitch, "Coaches Shouldn't Teach History."

[175] Jason Hill and Christina Stearns, Education and Certification Qualifications of Departmentalized Public High School-Level Teachers of Selected Subjects: Evidence From the 2011–12 Schools and Staffing Survey, National Center for Education Statistics, June, 2015 31. https://nces.ed.gov/pubs2015/2015814.pdf.

[176] Ibid., 19, 21.

courses.[177] With so little civics actually required in middle and high school, it is also the case that teachers assigned to teach it will often have other course responsibilities to round out their teaching load, making it all the more difficult to develop deep expertise.

To make matters worse, many teachers are required or pushed to major in education, some continuing their studies to obtain a master's degree in schools of education. Education degrees, however, are often not about what to teach but rather about how to teach. They are about pedagogy, not content. Teacher certification requirements across the fifty states are uneven at best. The authors of one 2015 study noted, "Only ten states have a pre-service certification requirement for high school civics or government teachers."[178] As a result, students are likely to end up in civics classes with teachers who are not fully prepared to teach that content.

If a number of teachers come to schools without the opportunity for adequate preparation, ongoing teacher development—on-the-job training—is left to cover the bases. Although there are professional development days on the job, the quality and effectiveness of this sort of education is spotty, at best. In a 2015 study of professional development opportunities in civic education, Rebecca Burgess reported several problems with

---

[177] Another survey in 2013 showed somewhat higher numbers, with 35 percent of civics teachers having majored in government or political science. Surbhi Godsay and Felicia M. Sullivan, "A National Survey of Civics and U.S. Government Teachers," Center for Information & Research on Civic Learning & Engagement, June 2014, 6. https://files.eric.ed.gov/fulltext/ED574357.pdf

[178] Peter Levine and Kei Kawashima-Ginsberg, "Civic Education and Deeper Learning," February 2015, 6.

such programs.[179] For one thing, there are too many subtopics in the field and too few professional development providers. For another, such programs are usually a menu of unconnected events and they end up emphasizing current events or civic engagement more than civic knowledge. It often requires a lot of initiative by teachers to find content-based programs in American history and government, generally provided by various nonprofits, and a fair bit of time and money to pursue them. Meanwhile, funding for content-based his*tory and civics professional development programs is precisely what has been cut in the last ten years.

Another common problem is that the education system too often doesn't value history and civics teachers appropriately. These are the people who, along with parents, are educating the next generation of citizens who will determine whether our American experiment in self-government survives. They should be the most valued of all educators. But are they? Just ask them. To get or keep a social studies job, for example, they often have to take on additional roles. There's an old joke among history and civics teachers we've heard over and over again: "Social studies teachers have a lot of last names, but only one first name: coach."[180] Perhaps the title of Ravitch's article overstates the issue, but it is nonetheless on to something: "Coaches Shouldn't Teach History."

---

[179] Rebecca Burgess, "Civic Education Professional Development: The Lay of the Land," American Enterprise Institute, March, 2015. https://files.eric.ed.gov/fulltext/ED557623.pdf

[180] John Fea, "History Teachers Who Did Not Study History in College," Current, September 21, 2015, https://currentpub.com/2015/09/21/history-teachers-who-did-not-study-history-in-college/.

What Does a Teacher Do in a Great American History and Civics Classroom?

So what does a teacher do to make a transformative experience for students in a history and civics classroom? Of course, every teacher will do things according to their own interests, tastes, and abilities. But, as educational researchers Russell Ackoff and Daniel Greenberg remind us, the best teachers understand that their classroom is not about teaching but about learning.[181] And the best history and civics teachers know that learning happens when they create conversation in their classroom about questions that matter to students as Americans and when they inspire wonder about what it means to be an American.

Create Conversation

Every great teacher does things their own way, so every great classroom will look different. Some are decorated; some are plain. Some are messy; some are neat. Some are loud; some are quiet.

But when a classroom has the kind of teacher we've discussed, it has a certain feel that is common to all great classrooms. It feels alive. There is an atmosphere of serious thinking, joyful discovery, and real relationships between the teachers and the students and among the students themselves. The relationship is partly personal: The teacher cares for the students because

---

[181] Knowledge at Wharton Staff, "'The Objective of Education Is Learning, Not Teaching,'" Knowledge at Wharton Podcast, August 20, 2008, 14:00, https://knowledge.wharton.upenn.edu/podcast/knowledge-at-wharton-podcast/the-objective-of-education-is-learning-not-teaching/

the teacher sees the beautiful potential in them to be human beings who can govern themselves as individuals and citizens. The students have affection, or at least respect, for the teacher because of how much the teacher knows about the subject and cares about them. But the friendship is more than personal—it is the bond produced by sharing a common high purpose in the pursuit of truth. The students and teacher sense that they are "in this together."

In American history and civics, this kind of classroom can only exist if it is centered on the two fundamental axioms of civic education: the mind is free, and America is free. In a classroom where the freedom of the mind is embraced, the teacher's role is not to give students information, but to cause them to think. And the best way to think is to do it out loud with others in conversation. A conversation is not a lecture; in a lecture, the speaker gives information to the listener, who more or less passively ingests it. The speaker might be energetic, enthusiastic, and even entertaining, so the listener might feel engaged with the speaker and even feel warmth for him. But the listener is not the equal of the speaker and is not free to speak (for example, the listener has to raise their hand to get permission from the speaker to ask a question or make a comment). Thus, there is still a distance between the person giving the information and the person receiving it. Conversation is also not debate. In a debate, both sides already know their conclusion and attempt to win the other (or the listeners) over to their opinion. Debate might be energetic, enthusiastic, and even entertaining, but there is a distance among those debating and between the debaters and listeners.

In contrast, conversation is intimate. "Conversation" comes from the Latin word *conversor*, which means "keep company with." In a conversation, people keep company with each other intellectually—ideas go back and forth and, hopefully, become more and more shared over time. People in a conversation draw closer to each other. Neither person is trying to win; they are considering an idea and thinking it through together as equals. This mutual exchange and coming together creates a respectful, perhaps even affectionate, bond between the interlocutors, even if they end up at different conclusions.

Inspire Wonder

Great teachers don't just create any kind of conversation—they create the kind that inspires wonder in their students. Wonder is not the same as confusion. Being confused means you have unclear or contradictory information in your head. Confusion is painful. People who are confused just want a clear answer. Wonder is the experience of realizing that you don't know the answer to a question that matters to you. Realizing you don't know what you thought you knew can be perplexing, but it is also pleasant because it liberates your mind to the exhilarating possibility of discovery. People in a state of wonder don't just want an answer; they want to find the truth, and they start asking questions and usually want to talk with others. As philosopher Jesse Prinz says, they become intellectually hungry.[182] For example, when you ask young Americans who care about their country what it means to be an American, they immediately care about the question. Or when you ask them why we should love

---

[182] Jesse Prinz, "How wonder works," ed. Ed Lake, Aeon, June 21, 2013, https://aeon.co/essays/why-wonder-is-the-most-human-of-all-emotions.

America, they care about the answer. When you show them that they don't actually know the answer to that question, they begin to wonder.

In an American history and civics classroom, a teacher can raise questions that cause wonder by using primary documents, not textbooks. Textbooks contain information that has been distilled in summary form for easy absorption. A student with deeper questions cannot dig below the surface of a textbook because there is, by design, nothing below the surface. Primary documents do not give summaries; they make arguments that have layers of depth that provide fuller and fuller answers as the reader digs deeper. You can ask a primary source a question, get an answer, and ask a further question. If a student wants to know what it means to be an American, they can read the Declaration of Independence and "talk" with Thomas Jefferson. They can ask him questions, and he will respond. Then they can ask him follow-up questions and get into a real conversation. All it takes is curiosity and imagination. Likewise, students can read the Gettysburg Address and engage with Abraham Lincoln. They can read the "I Have a Dream" speech and converse with Martin Luther King Jr. In other words, a student can have a conversation with a primary document that draws them closer to the mind of the author and the historical events of his time. To some people, this description might sound too good to be true, but anyone who has been in a great history and civics classroom knows that it can happen. Our job is to help teachers make it happen.

Creating Great History and Civics Teachers

Helping people become those kinds of teachers requires returning to basic principles. We agree with Ravitch that "[o]ur young people should study history with teachers who love history, who can go far beyond the textbook to get youngsters involved in learning about the exciting events and controversies that bring history to life; we need teachers who know enough about history to awaken the curiosity of their students and to encourage them to read more than the textbooks tell them and even to question what the textbooks tell them."[183] These kinds of people know American history and government, love American history and government, and love helping students discover it for themselves. They have deep knowledge and contagious enthusiasm. They understand the fundamental documents and debates that have defined who we are as Americans. They realize the urgent need to educate the next generation of informed patriots. And they are valued for their educational knowledge and civic importance.

How do we get these kinds of American history and civics teachers? In general, we need to do four things: first, attract the best people to the job; second, educate them in the fundamental documents, principles, and history that they need to know; third, give them the freedom to teach what they know and love; and fourth, treat them like the important professionals they are.

---

[183] Ravitch, "Coaches Shouldn't Teach History."

Talent

First, if we want great civic education, we need to attract the best talent possible into history and civics teaching. A number of countries like Finland have had real success in K–12 education because they admit only the best and brightest as teachers.[184] Arthur Levine, the emeritus president of Teachers College at Columbia University, found that "[i]n such high-achieving countries as Singapore, South Korea, and Finland, admission to a teacher training program is highly competitive. Only students in the top 10-20% of their high school or college cohort are admitted to an elementary or secondary training program."[185] Unfortunately, that's not true in America. As Katharine Boles and Vivian Trn note, "[t]eacher education programs around the country are caught in a bind. They have to fill their seats in order to run programs that are economically viable. If their standards for admission are set too high, they won't be able to fill the seats they have. This problem affects the selection and quality of the candidates in most of the nation's teacher education programs."[186] Ravitch argues that "[m]any states recognize that they must make extraordinary efforts to reach out and recruit qualified teachers of physical sciences, but there is no comparable

[184] "Why is a Finnish Education Better? It's All About Teachers," Tenney School, December 7, 2016, https://tenneyschool.com/why-is-a-finnish-education-better-its-all-about-teachers/.

[185] Sandra Stotsky, "Why Do Education Schools Have Such Low Standards?," Minding the Campus, January 24, 2013, https://www.mindingthecampus.org/2013/01/24/why_do_education_schoolshave_s/.

[186] News editor, "Why The Teacher Crisis is Worse Than You Think (And What Can Be Done About It)," Harvard Graduate School of Education, June 1, 2003, https://www.gse.harvard.edu/news/03/06/why-teacher-crisis-worse-you-think-and-what-can-be-done-about-it.

awareness of the conspicuous need for such teachers in social studies."[187]

So how do we get even more talented people into history and civics teaching? One way is to hire middle and high school teachers in the same way university professors are hired: anyone with the talent to teach should be eligible to teach. That is already happening at many private schools around the country, as they do not necessarily require certified teachers with a bachelor's degree in education. They just need to know the subject matter and have the ability to create conversation and spark wonder in young people. Principals and hiring committees of experienced teachers can make a judgment about whether someone has the talent.

This would mean abolishing or, at the very least, modifying teacher certification and licensure requirements. Omri Ben-Shahar, a law professor at the University of Chicago, argues that "[a]bolishing certification requirements is not only virtually costless, but it would eliminate the onerous costs certification exacts. And it offers the best hope of bringing more capable people into the teaching that all agree is so vital."[188] At the very least, states should further open up alternative licensure or certification for teachers. In 2022, *Education Week* reported that the movement had already begun: "Across the country, policymakers are taking steps to relax their states' certification requirements to get more teachers in the classroom and circumvent shortages…. [A]

---

[187] Ravitch, "Coaches Shouldn't Teach History."

[188] Omri Ben-Shahar and Carl E. Schneider, "Teacher Certification Makes Public School Education Worse, Not Better," Forbes, July 21, 2017, https://www.forbes.com/sites/omribenshahar/2017/07/21/teacher-certification-makes-public-school-education-worse-not-better/?sh=8bb-b1a4730fe

bout a dozen states have recently amended—or are considering amending—teacher certification rules. Some are changing the criteria for licensure, others are expanding the qualifying score on state licensing tests, and some are dropping licensure tests altogether." But more could be done. As mentioned above, we need to give experienced principals and teachers the freedom to hire talented teachers regardless of whether they have a teaching degree, license, or certification.[189] And if those people prove to be effective teachers, they should not be required to acquire any license or certification. Great teaching *is* their license.

Content Education

Second, we need teachers who have a deep education in the content of American history and government, because you cannot truly teach what you do not truly know. Right now, as Diane Ravitch noted, many or even most middle and high school history and civics teachers have a bachelor's degree in "education," not in their subject area.[190] They take courses in the subject areas like history and government, but they also take many education theory and pedagogy classes, sometimes even more than the content courses. Ravitch argues that "the shortage of qualified teachers of history…is one created by short-sighted state policies, which put more emphasis on pedagogical degrees than on knowledge of one's subject. The young person with a history degree who wants to teach may be required to take many courses

---

189 https://www0.gsb.columbia.edu/faculty/jrockoff/certification-final.pdf
190 Ravitch, "Coaches Shouldn't Teach History."

in pedagogy, even another master's degree in pedagogy, whether relevant to teaching ability or not."[191]

So how do we get such knowledgeable teachers? Again, the example of other countries can be helpful. Sandra Slotsky, emeritus professor of educational research at the University of Arkansas, notes:

> All prospective teachers in Finland...must have graduated from an academic high school.... Prospective subject teachers usually complete a three-year B.A. degree program and two-year master's program in their subject in the arts and sciences, followed by a two-year master's program in education.... [S]ubject teachers are supervised by faculty with joint appointments in the arts and sciences and pedagogy. In both models subject teachers are expected to have a deep understanding of their subject before they begin their teaching career, and in their pedagogical training they are not separated from discipline-based faculty.[192]

The key is that even when studying pedagogy, content mastery should always be the most important part of their education as teachers.

In the American context, we can get teachers who are masters of the content of American history and government by requiring them to hold an undergraduate, or perhaps even a graduate,

---

[191] Ibid.
[192] Stotsky, "Why Do Education Schools."

degree in history and/or political science. But even then, it cannot be an ordinary history or political science degree. It needs to be centered on the study of primary source documents and great texts. To ask questions that spark wonder and guide a meaningful conversation about the Constitution, teachers cannot just know merely superficial information about the Constitution. They must have studied the Constitution's text itself as well as *The Federalist* and the writings of the Anti-Federalists, and they must have read James Madison's *Notes on the Constitutional Convention*. Only with this kind of knowledge can they help their students understand that the Constitution was controversial and be able to recreate the original debates over it. To teach the story of the Civil War, a teacher must have studied Alexander Stephens's "Cornerstone Speech," the Mississippi Resolution on Secession, Lincoln's First Inaugural Address, the Emancipation Proclamation, the Gettysburg Address, and Lincoln's Second Inaugural Address. We would venture to say that most middle and high school history teachers did not study these documents in their undergraduate education programs. Unfortunately, as the American Council of Trustees and Alumni has shown, most history majors in college don't study them either: "less than 1/3 of the nations leading colleges and universities require students pursuing a degree in history to take a single course in American history."[193]

---

[193] American Council of Trustees and Alumni (ACTA), "No U.S. History?," July 1, 2016, https://www.goacta.org/resource/no_u-s-_history/.

Freedom to Teach and State Social Studies Standards

Finally, we need teachers with the freedom to teach the defining documents and debates of America. While some districts or individual schools tightly prescribe and monitor the textbook or other resources that teachers use in their classroom, it is often true in practice that teachers have surprising freedom to supplement or even put aside the textbook. What is true in practice should be true in principle. If teachers have serious, content-based education, they can be trusted to choose the best primary source curriculum for their classroom.

The choice of a curriculum, however, often flows downstream from a state's social studies standards. The National Association of Scholars argues:

> State standards are the single most influential documents in America's education system. State education departments use them to provide guidance to each public K–12 school district and charter school as they create their own courses. State standards also influence what textbook authors write and what assessment companies such as the College Board test for in their advanced placement examinations. They affect teacher training and they provide the framework for teachers' individual lesson plans. Private schools and homeschool parents also keep an eye on state standards.[194]

---

[194] "American Birthright: The Civics Alliance's Model K-12 Social Studies Standards," Civics Alliance, https://civicsalliance.org/american-birthright/.

Ileana Najarro, an education writer, confirms that "[s]ocial studies standards help guide instruction in the classroom, both in terms of what content to cover and how to do so. State boards of education typically oversee the process of drafting and approving new standards."[195] Sometimes, those standards are set by the state legislature in some detail; usually, as Navarro notes, the standards are created by state boards of education, state departments of education, or other administrative agencies.[196]

Unfortunately, state history and civics standards too often fall into one of two categories: overly prescriptive or muddled. Unfortunately, both deficiencies result in the same problem: students do not focus on the most important questions, documents, and debates that define America. On the prescriptive side, state standards require teachers to "cover everything," forcing them to rush through important material and rely on textbooks for information. They cannot really distinguish between the important and less important. Class becomes a race to transmit as much information as possible in as short a time as possible rather than a serious conversation that actually causes students to wonder and discover. No wonder students and teachers find it exhausting and boring.

Muddled standards do not provide the clarity needed to focus attention on what is important. As the Thomas B. Fordham Institute says, unclear standards "[p]rovide overbroad, vague, or otherwise insufficient guidance for curriculum and

---

195 Ileana Najarro, "Writing Social Studies Standards: A (Dramatic) Year in Review," Education Week, December 23, 2022, https://www.edweek.org/teaching-learning/writing-social-studies-standards-a-dramatic-year-in-review/2022/12.

196 Stern et al., "The State of State Standards."

instruction," "[o]mit or seriously underemphasize topics that are essential to informed citizenship and historical comprehension," "[m]ake poor use of the early grades or fail to revisit essential content in later grades," and "[p]ay little attention to writing, argumentation, problem analysis, and the connections between core content and current issues and events."[197] In a 2021 study conducted by the Fordham Institute on state history and civics standards, only:

> ...five jurisdictions received "exemplary" ratings...in both subjects: Alabama, California, Massachusetts, Tennessee, and the District of Columbia (New York's U.S. History standards are also "exemplary"). Another ten states, led by Georgia, Oklahoma, and Virginia, received "good" ratings...in both subjects. Three states (Texas, Ohio, and Louisiana) were deemed "good" in one subject but "mediocre" in the other. Eight states were rated "mediocre" in both subjects. Four states were rated "mediocre" in one subject and "inadequate" in the other. Finally, twenty states were rated "inadequate," meaning they received "D" or "F" grades in both subjects.[198]

While the Fordham Institute ratings are helpful, to truly improve standards we need to move to a different model: an inquiry-based framework for the layer-cake approach we

---

[197] Ibid.
[198] Ibid.

described earlier. This means that while American history and civics content builds on itself from the earliest grades up through high school, the content itself is framed by important questions that persist across grade levels and whose answers are found more and more in primary texts as students move into middle and high school. For example, the common framing question of American history and civics standards should be: "What does it mean to be an American?" The standards for each grade would be framed by that question, with sub-questions derived from it guiding the content of each grade. For example, "What is the common 'creed' of America, according to Martin Luther King Jr.?"

In recent years, there has been some movement toward inquiry-based standards. For example, the Educating for American Democracy (EAD) Roadmap is inquiry-based and seeks to promote that approach for state standards.[199] As its own report says, "[a]t its core, the Roadmap to Educating for American Democracy focuses on the value of the inquiry process and reasonable discourse that encourages the exploration of open-ended questions…. The EAD Roadmap makes the case—and provides guidance—for inquiry as an effective method for high-quality teaching and learning."[200] The advantage of inquiry-based standards is that they provide districts and teachers with a helpful focus but also allow teachers the freedom to slow down and focus on what is truly important. Teachers can take the time to have real conversations with

---

[199] "Learn to read the Roadmap," Educating for American Democracy, https://www.educatingforamericandemocracy.org/the-roadmap/#state-standards.
[200] Ibid.

their students. And they can tailor the curriculum to best suit the needs of their classroom.

Unfortunately, however, the EAD Roadmap does not solve our state standards problem. While the Roadmap is intended to inform state standards, it is explicitly not a set of history and civics standards. As Stoner and Carrese say, EAD "aims to provide a roadmap—not a comprehensive national curriculum, but a list of topics deserving attention, and of critical questions that ought to be asked."[201] Stoner and Carrese continue by noting that "[t]he EAD aimed to…leav[e] curriculum developers and individual teachers in the 50 states the freedom to design their own routes, so to speak."[202]

And we agree that EAD should not supply the framework for state standards. As we noted previously, the EAD Roadmap says that it is the product of "over 300 academics, historians, educators, and other experts, individuals with very different perspectives and backgrounds," who came together "with the goal of issuing guidance for excellence in K–12 U.S. history and civics instruction, and doing so with consensus."[203] Inevitably, to reach consensus among people with so many different and even disparate views, many compromises had to be made, including on critical questions. For example, does EAD recommend action

---

[201] James R. Stoner Jr. and Paul O. Carrese, "What's So Un-American about a Shared American Civics?," National Review, June 9, 2021, https://www.nationalreview.com/2021/06/whats-so-un-american-about-a-shared-american-civics/.

[202] Ibid.

[203] "Seeking a Truce in the Civics & History Wars: Is 'Educating for American Democracy' the Answer?," Thomas B. Fordham Institute, June 28, 2021, https://fordhaminstitute.org/national/events/seeking-truce-civics-history-wars-educating-american-democracy-answer.

civics? While the EAD Roadmap does not openly tout action civics, Stanley Kurtz, a critic of EAD, argues:

> ...the EAD report is notable for burying the most politically charged and significant issues in its various appendices. They are by far the most interesting and revealing parts of the report.... "Appendix C" of the EAD report.... endorses action civics, along with companion practices such as "service learning" (required internships with political advocacy groups), and teacher-led discussions of current political and social controversies, calling them all "proven practices." According to the report, these concepts are "woven into" and "reflected in the EAD Roadmap and its Pedagogy Companion." So, rather than being some parenthetical point of little relevance to the roadmap (or other EAD documents), the appendix is telling us that action civics and its companion practices pervade the vaunted roadmap, and other EAD products as well.[204]

Given the limitations of the EAD Roadmap and the problems with state standards, we believe that it is vital to create a new, inquiry-based set of American history and civics standards that can serve as a model for the states. These standards should prescribe clear and compelling questions that frame a

---

[204] Stanley Kurtz, "Consensus by Surrender," National Review, June 10, 2021, https://www.nationalreview.com/corner/consensus-by-surrender/.

layer-cake K–12 curriculum; the questions should focus on the important documents and debates that have defined America; in addressing those questions, the standards should not try to "get through everything" but should instead embrace the freedom of teachers to slow down and study the most important things; and the standards should be able to be used in the full range of classrooms with wide variety of students, from remedial to International Baccalaureate high achievers. This effort has already begun in some quarters. For example, the Civics Alliance, led by the National Association of Scholars, has put out its "American Birthright" standards for American history and civics. While deserving study, these standards are not inquiry-based and thus would not, in our view, serve as a model set of standards—at least not without some important revision. We call on leaders in civic education to embark on this critical endeavor as soon as possible.

Conclusion

As we have said, there are three essential elements to strong history and civics classrooms: rigorous, inquiry-based state standards; primary source curriculum; and content-based teacher education. Inquiry-based standards are important because they focus civic education on the most important and engaging questions of America. Primary source curriculum is vital because it allows students to dig deep into those questions. But the most important element is teachers. Standards are just pieces of paper unless they are put into action by a teacher. Curriculum is just words on a page until a teacher brings it to life. Even if the standards are bad and the curriculum is subpar, it is possible to have good civic education with a great teacher. So if we are going to restore civic education in America, we must start with K–12 teachers of American history and civics. Because of the depth and breadth of their impact, these teachers are the most important factor in determining whether students actually learn what they need in order to be capable of preserving self-government in America.

To have great teachers, we need talented people who have the content education and classroom freedom to inspire curiosity and wonder in their students. It is time to move away from educating teachers in "how" to teach more than "what" to teach. It is time to move away from a focus on lectures derived from textbooks to conversations about the story of America based on the primary documents of our country. And it is time to realize that American history and civics teachers have the most important job in K–12 education.

CHAPTER SIX

More and Better: The Keys to Improving Civic Education

When we study a problem, we tend to look through a particular lens—one that we are familiar with, one that we know how to use. The old aphorism contains a lot of truth: "To a hammer, everything looks like a nail." Or, as a psychologist friend used to say when someone would try to tell him what his own problems were, "Don't go assigning your favorite motive to my actions." We use our way of looking at the world as the right way to diagnose anyone's problems, including those of the society at large.

To some degree, this is happening now with civic education. While there is a growing recognition that civic education is in a trough and in need of strengthening and improving, everyone seems to have their own theory about how we got there and why it is important to address it. An education historian might look at civic education over time and say that it has waxed and waned at different periods, so we are simply in a natural cycle of waning interest. Some conservatives might see the loss of emphasis on

JEFFREY SIKKENGA AND DAVID DAVENPORT

civic education as part of a liberal plot to undermine American traditions and values. Many liberals considered the election of Donald Trump and the rise of populism as evidence that we need more civic education. The contemporary social justice movement would point out that the civic education we have is wrong-headed, teaching antiquated narratives about American history and values.

We admit we have a point of view also, that of educators who want to see civic education cultivate the next generation of informed patriots. Our perspective is that just as we would not want uneducated scientists doing our research or poorly educated doctors performing surgery, we do not want the next generation of citizens and leaders to be turned loose on the American republic without civic training. This seems like a more hopeful starting point than some others, because we need not argue about how to use civic education to change the world, as others seek to do. Everyone will have a different opinion about that. Understanding there are difficult complexities down the road, we want to start the journey at a simpler point, namely by asking how we can strengthen civic education.

To us, improving civic education boils down to two basic ideas: *more* and *better*. The need for *more* civic education is both obvious and a goal around which people with different points of view could rally. We need *more* civic education at home (as Ronald Reagan put it, around the dinner table). We need *more* in elementary and middle school, where history and civics have too often given way to other subjects. We need *more* than just a single one-semester government course in high school. We need *more* in teacher education and in colleges and universities. We need *more* civic education fostered by community organizations.

Our first set of recommendations for strengthening civic education is simply this: more, more, and more.

Second, we need *better* civic education. We understand there will be arguments here about the exact content of civic education, and political agendas are likely to raise their heads. Still, we think it is possible to reach some agreement on what educational approaches will lead to the best possible teaching of civic education. Our students, and our country, deserve no less.

More

The Role of the Family
When a president of the United States leaves office, he sometimes offers an important message. George Washington's Farewell Address, for example, is thought of as one of his most significant speeches. In more modern times, Dwight Eisenhower left behind a warning about the growing role of "the military-industrial complex." In his farewell speech, Ronald Reagan chose to emphasize the importance of citizenship and civics. He spoke of the need for "an informed patriotism" among America's citizens, noting that "all great change in America begins at the dinner table." Reagan felt it was vital for the future that parents share with their kids "what it means to be an American."

We begin our recommendations for more civic education, then, at that same place: in the family. For here, it is more than merely education, it is a set of roots that can be planted deeper into the young soil of children's lives. It helps children know that America, not just as a country but as a set of ideas and ideals, is an important part of family identity. It lays a base on which the later school teaching of history and civics takes on greater value and importance.

How to do this? Let us count the ways. Simply talking about America and its stories is one important way. In our families, we were happy when our parents read to us but even happier when they told us stories. Reading stories to children about America and some of its heroes and holidays is another great way to introduce them to civic education. Even discussing current events at their level can be a valuable connection to civics and history. Taking children along on civic and political outings—whether to vote or to a rally—can help them see the importance of this in the family. Summer field trips can easily include teachable moments by visits to national parks, monuments, battlefields and the like. Since values are better caught than taught, modeling educated citizenship for children is itself a crucial role for parents.

Elementary School

As noted earlier, civics has all but been lost in the elementary school curriculum. As in the family and home, however, the early grades are the time to plant the roots of civic interest and importance. To the extent that politicization has become a problem in teaching civics, it can, and should, be less of a problem in these early grades, allowing a greater consensus for more civic education in grade schools. In fact, we would go a step further and suggest that starting with an objective but positive frame about America's story is important in these early years. We agree with Ross Douthat, writing in the *New York Times*, that if we love our country as we might love family—flaws and all—"you probably want to feel a certain security in your children's family bonds before you start telling them about every sin and scandal."[205] So in the elementary years, we should be laying a proper base for civic education.

We advocate the layer-cake approach to the teaching of civic education: we start in kindergarten with a base layer that is age-appropriate, and we build on that in every grade as students are able to understand and handle more. A recent study by the Thomas B. Fordham Institute refers to this favorably as "effective scaffolding," building a framework by learning some things earlier that allow for more complex learning later.[206] Schools do that in most core subjects such as math, reading, and science, and it would be equally easy and appropriate to construct such a curriculum for civic education. That way, by the time students reach the comprehensive high school course that focuses on the history and especially the principles of our country (the "why" of America), they have a context, a vocabulary, and a broad understanding of many of the concepts. Otherwise, a one-semester high school course easily becomes too little, too late.

Unfortunately, there is a long way to go here, with all social studies receiving only 10 percent of class time per week in elementary school—by far the least of any core subject.[207] A number of states have moved toward requiring more civics in elementary school, primarily by designating civics and US his-

---

[205] Ross Douthat, "Why A Patriotic Education Can Be Valuable," New York Times, July 10, 2021, https://www.nytimes.com/2021/07/10/opinion/sunday/history-education-patriotic.html.

[206] Stern et al., "The State of State Standards."

[207] "The Marginalization of Social Studies," Council of Chief State School Officers, November 16, 2018, https://ccsso.org/resource-library/marginalization-social-studies.

tory subject matter that should be covered in each grade. The Fordham Institute study referenced earlier does a comprehensive job of reviewing and grading each state's approach to this in both K–8 grades as well as in high school.[208] A few states do well in the Fordham Institute study, though many are rated poorly. In particular, the approaches taken by Maryland and Florida are quite comprehensive and specific, engaging students with important topics and quality material in civics and history from kindergarten on.

Increasing the time spent and topics taught on civics and history in elementary school would be a highly leveraged (and less political) way to strengthen civic education. In the previous chapter, we called on leaders in civic education to create model, inquiry-based standards for states to consider for all grades, including elementary school. In the meantime, state boards of education should study some of the best standards and begin to move in that direction. For reasons already discussed, we are not in favor of more federal spending on K–12 education, but if the federal government were to provide additional funding for civic education, investment at the elementary school level would be a good way to go. All this will also require additional teacher education since so little has been done in these areas in recent years. States should require that the NAEP test in US history and civics be given in the fourth grade as well as the eighth grade, thereby fortifying the emphasis on civic education in the elementary school years.

---

[208] Stern et al., "The State of State Standards."

Middle School

Civic education in middle school reflects some of the uncertainty of the curriculum in middle school generally. There seems to be more consensus on what we do in elementary and high school, but middle school, also known as junior high school, is still a bit of an in-between set of grades. A few states have begun to increase civic education standards in middle school, but most have done very little.

Since the middle school curriculum is generally less prescribed than high school, it would seem to be a good opportunity to do more with the civic education. In fact, the Fordham Institute study of state standards in civics and history says just that: "In general, states with 'exemplary' civics standards see the middle grades as an opportunity...."[209] Massachusetts, for example, requires middle school students to complete a civics project. In Indiana, the "We the People" program engages middle school students in a competition to judge their understanding of constitutional principles.[210] Most states teach primarily history (as opposed to civics per se) in the middle school years, though even there, important groundwork can be laid and connections drawn for civic education.

A few states have decided to add a civic education course to the middle school curriculum. Florida was an early adopter of such a one-semester course, and it has seen improvement in its civics test scores. Alabama and Indiana have such courses in middle school, and New Jersey added such a requirement beginning

---

[209] Ibid.
[210] See "We the People," Indiana Bar Foundation, https://www.inbarfoundation.org/we-the-people/.

in the fall of 2022. We commend states that have required such courses as an effective way to continue to build the layer cake of civic understanding, pointing toward the more comprehensive and standard course in civic education in high school.

Middle school, specifically the eighth grade, is when the NAEP government and US history tests have been given in recent years, and states should be provided and utilize data from these tests as one possible way to measure the effectiveness of civic education in their jurisdiction.

High School

It's difficult to believe that not every state requires at least a one-semester high school course in civic education. It would seem to be the absolute minimum a state should do, and yet, we are still several states short of 100 percent—a gap that simply must be closed. Turning students loose into adulthood without a solid and focused grounding in the principles and institutions of America does a disservice to them as well as to the republic they should be prepared to serve.

Beyond that bare minimum, however, there are a couple of other ways to increase the emphasis on civic education in high school. One would be to require a full year of government and civics, not just a single semester. Such a course would need to include attention to the primary documents and texts of the American Founding, especially since many states do not require a high school history course in the Founding. As noted earlier, the heavy emphasis on STEM education has resulted in a great increase in science and math requirements and courses, mostly at the expensive of the humanities and social sciences, including civic education. While math and science may be helpful in securing jobs, civic education is important to securing our democracy. With school requirements covering everything from science and math to physical education and languages, surely we could carve out a full year of study in government to prepare young people to take up the duties of citizenship.

Another way to increase the emphasis on civic education in high schools is through testing. At a minimum, states should require the NAEP tests on US history and government, now administered only in the eighth grade, in the twelfth grade as well. Other tests may also prove helpful. For example, a number of states have begun requiring that students pass the civics portion of the same citizenship test as immigrants seeking citizenship must do. Although reducing civic education to a single test is not, in our view, ideal educationally, nevertheless it does require that coursework prepare students for the test. Indeed, there is research showing that such testing does improve educational outcomes.[211] If nothing else, perhaps such testing should be considered in the early days of a civic education revival, with the possibility of removing these "training wheels" later when NAEP test scores show significant progress in mastering the subject.

---

[211] David E. Campbell, "Putting Civics to the Test: The Impact of State-Level Civics Assessments On Civic Knowledge," AEI Research, September 17, 2014, https://www.aei.org/wp-content/uploads/2014/11/2014-09-Campbell.final-template.pdf.

Bipartisan Improvements

While there may be disagreement and even political battles over how civic education is taught, there is real progress to be made by addressing how much it is taught. *More* civic education need not be—indeed, should not be—controversial. Even if nothing else can be agreed to, beginning to build civic knowledge and interest in the elementary grades should be one of the highest priorities. This begins building the layer cake of civic education that is so essential to improvement. Then, we should look for special opportunities to add more civics—not just American history—to the middle school curriculum. The gold standard would be joining those few states who now require a civics course in middle school. Then, the high school course, which should be expanded to a full year, becomes the icing on the layer cake, filling out our responsibility to prepare students with an adequate civic education. Job number-one for improving civic education is *more*.

Better Civic Education

People will differ on how to improve civic education. To a large extent, one's ideas on how to make civic education better will depend on what they think the current problems are in the teaching of the subject, as well as their own views on what they want civic education to achieve. For example, many believe that civic education has become too boring and too oriented toward rote memorization of dates and systems. Often, their solution is to abandon civic knowledge as a priority and turn instead to action civics. But, as we have noted earlier, that's a kind of cut-flower civics with no real roots to sustain it. There are ways to teach civic knowledge that are interesting to students, and we ought not give up on that as a primary goal.

Another school of thought that has come to the fore of late is the notion that many of the problems with America's republic could be solved with a different approach to civic education. To the extent that some believe America is infected by racial and social injustice, for example, their solution involves a different way of teaching US history and civics with much greater emphasis on slavery and inequality. Of course, this way of reforming civic education runs headlong into traditionalists who believe that young people need a grounding in what has made America exceptional more than what makes it ill-founded or unjust.

Although threading our way through these philosophical and political minefields is tricky business, our view is that there are ways people can agree on that would make the teaching of civic education better. For example, we believe civic education should be an "all hands on deck" project, not just a school curriculum. Civic education needs to be embraced and encouraged in families and civic associations and by government and other leaders in our society. It needs to be understood as a high priority for the nation, embraced and encouraged by everyone. Civic education needs to be "caught" as well as "taught."

A best practice that everyone should be able to embrace educationally is the layer-cake recipe for civic education. We start with the base layer in the family, preschool, and elementary years by teaching the core values and practices of our democratic republic. Why and how do we salute the flag? Who were some of the American heroes, and what were their stories? Why do we celebrate certain holidays that have a civic purpose? Where did the national anthem come from? These are all things that kids will encounter in their lives and they present natural opportunities to begin their civic education. With each grade, then, we add more age-appropriate layers to the civic education cake, right on through the major high school civics course. This is a way to do better civic education that should have strong appeal.

Another way to do better civic education is to pay heed to the pedagogical questions raised in chapter four. Like most subjects, civic education is best introduced with the "what" questions that are so basic to understanding everything else. At the elementary school level, the "why" questions should be included, but they should be present through stories rather than deep discussions of primary texts. Then as students grow older and have stronger powers of reasoning, the "how" questions become more pertinent. Finally, a good civic education prompts to students to ask and think about "why" our democratic republic works as it does. We fundamentally agree with those who say that reducing civic education to memorizing a bunch of dates and events shoots way too low on the educational quality target. Although addressing the deeper "why" questions requires a base of civic knowledge, those are the questions that excite and motivate students to become better citizens—which is after all, the real goal of civic education.

As we have argued in chapters four and five, we believe using primary documents to teach civics and history leads to better civic education. Textbooks are often boring at best and biased at their worst. They can lead to political controversy over what to include and exclude. They tend to stay with the lower level "what" or "how" questions without really addressing the "why." They also risk the problem of presentism: by bringing the past to us rather than making us go to the past, we continue to wear our twenty-first-century glasses to understand the people and issues of a different time. Far better is to ask students to remove those glasses and travel back in time to read important speeches, debates, laws, and documents and study events of the time. This approach to teaching history and government creates far more excitement as students learn and debate the issues of that time. It helps them see how the republic works under the stresses and strains of poverty, war, disease, division, and other challenges. And, most importantly, it invites students to draw their own conclusions—not those of a textbook author or teacher. This is civic education at its finest.

Yet another valuable way to get to better civic education is to provide better teacher education. Since teachers are the heart of the learning enterprise, their ability and knowledge is a highly leveraged place to invest. As noted in chapter four, teachers in history and government often have not had the opportunity to be as well prepared and credentialed in their subject as they would like and need. Then, too, if we begin offering new courses and emphases in several grades, additional teacher education and development will be needed. Eventually, schools of education and state accreditation standards will need to respond to the need for better education, but, in the meantime, further investments in professional development, and the nonprofit organizations that provide it, will be important.

Finally, better—and less politically controversial—civic education could be built on principles of federalism. That is to say, we should allow each level of the process to play its own proper role, without other players reaching in to try to take control or fix things. For example, the federal government should be primarily a cheerleader for civic education, perhaps a funder, but it should not be a player in what is taught and how. Education is not a federal responsibility—that belongs to others. Washington,

DC, is quite simply the wrong place for debates and bills specifying what should be taught as civic education and how it should be taught. Those should be hands off in Congress and the Department of Education.

State legislatures have a vital but limited responsibility. Their job is to decide how much civic education should be required in their schools and in which grades. Recently a few states have begun to take that responsibility more seriously but, as the 2021 Fordham Institute study of state standards shows, most states are not at all where they should be in requirements and standards for US history and civics. Legislatures need to leave the particulars of whether this or that idea should be taught or what approach should be used to teachers and schools and focus on job number-one for them: making certain that there are high standards and strong requirements in all grades for the teaching of civic education.

Schools and teachers, then, are left to decide how to teach and, to some degree, what to teach. Some will complain that this leaves too much variation around the country in what students are taught. But this has always been so in our federal republic. Recognizing that values and needs are different, Utah does not have to do what New York does, for example, nor does California have to follow the dictates of Alabama. Similarly, educators in one school or district will make different decisions than another. Still, these educational questions need to be worked out at the level closest to the action by school districts, schools, and teachers.

We hope we have shown that, even with strong disagreements about the politics of civic education, agreement can be built around better ways to do it: building a layer cake of civic knowledge and education from kindergarten to twelfth grade by implementing age-appropriate methods at each level, using primary documents to create both more engagement in the classroom and better results on testing, and providing *more* and *better* teacher education. And, by way of process, American federalism can return decisions to the places and levels that are best prepared to deal with them.

Putting Principles into Practice

It's one thing to think more clearly about the need for more and better civic education, but we are at the point where urgent action is needed. Most of us make to-do lists for our jobs and even our personal lives, so let us close with to-do lists for improving civic education. We offer one each for the two groups most able to influence and improve civic education: educators and policy-makers.

To-Do List for Educators

Philosophy:
1. Embrace civic education as a top educational priority throughout the curriculum of all grades.
2. Understand that the purpose of civic education is ultimately to develop "informed patriots" who understand why—despite its shortcomings—America deserves their love and active engagement in order to preserve and improve its institutions and civic life.
3. Embrace the principle that "civic education" is made up of both American history and government, which go hand-in-hand.

4. Base civic education on the idea that America was founded on principles of freedom and that our history is the story of our struggle to live up to those principles.

5. Look for other opportunities to weave civic education into the school day and year. Tie civic education in with holidays, songs, the news, reading assignments in other subjects, etc.

Standards and Curricula:

1. Make civic education standards "inquiry-based" and focus on the most important questions that define America. These questions should frame the American history and government curriculum across grade levels. The most important question is: "What does it mean to be an American?"

2. Begin curricula and standards with the "what" questions of civic education but, as students mature, challenge them to think about the "how" and, most important, the "why" questions.

3. Do not force the standards to cover everything in every historical period. Focus on the important questions that tell the story of America and leave time and freedom for teachers to focus on in-depth study of documents and creation of projects.

4. Build a curriculum layer cake of civic education beginning in the earliest grades, adding more complex material to the cake as students advance through the grades. Think of the high school course as the top layer, not the whole cake.

Teaching Methods:

1. Do not indoctrinate or simply transmit information. Rather, prompt thinking and wonder in the students by asking questions and encouraging them to pursue the truth and draw their own conclusions.
2. Engage students in conversation, not just lecture.
3. Use primary documents, not just textbooks. Challenge students to see history and government through the eyes and experiences of earlier generations, not just through twenty-first-century lenses. Primary documents take students into critical moments in the development of the American experiment, humanizing history, and bringing it to life. Considerable material for this is available at www.tah.org.
4. Embrace the opportunity to convey your own love of country, with its rich history and highly developed political system. Such values are often better caught than taught.

K–12 History and Civics Teacher Development:

1. Provide opportunities for teachers to avail themselves of content-based, primary source–driven professional development.
2. Support the many nonprofits that offer excellent teacher development opportunities and tools.

To-Do List for Policy Makers

The policy makers who matter most in K–12 education, including civic education, are state legislators and state and local school boards. Ultimately, they are the ones who decide what schools are required to do about civic education. Therefore, our to-do list is addressed to them.

Before we offer that action list, however, a brief word to federal policy makers is in order. As we have emphasized, education is a state and local matter, not a federal one. The federal government has no constitutional role in telling schools what or how to teach. What, then, should the federal government do, if anything, about civic education? First and foremost, it should be a cheerleader, lending the influential voices of senior government leaders to the growing consensus about the need for more and better civic education. As we noted earlier, this is one of those "Sputnik moments," when we collectively recognize the urgency to improve some part of education, and the federal government should help rally the troops and support the movement.

Beyond lending its voice, the federal government may choose to provide some funding. As noted earlier, this is always tricky because federal funding often comes with strings attached, providing not only money but also direction about how the money should be spent. If the federal government chooses to offer additional funding to civic education, there are several guidelines that could prevent unwarranted federal intrusion into the substance of civic education. First, it could offer the money as block grants to states, clearly empowering the states to make the spending decisions. Second, the federal government could jump-start a part of civic education that is behind, namely support for teaching the subject in elementary schools. Third, it could provide funding for teacher education and development, something that is needed across the board.

Finally, there is one thing the federal government could do to be helpful in funding civic education. It could offer financial incentives to states to expand the administration of the US history and government NAEP tests to be widely administered in the fourth and twelfth grades, along with the eighth grade as it is now offered. Thorough data about performance on the test should be provided to each state, so that policymakers and educators will have the data necessary to implement additional efforts and improvements where needed.

If state legislators or school board members were to ask us what they should be doing about civic education, here is the to-do list we would offer them:

To-Do List for State Policymakers

Require More Coursework:

1. Establish a robust set of civic education requirements spanning from kindergarten through high school. Civic education should be part of the curriculum in every grade.
2. Require American history and government throughout the elementary and middle school years. In high school, require a total of at least three years of American history and government, including at least one semester of study on the American Founding (the Declaration of Independence, the US Constitution, and so on).

Provide More Teacher Education:

1. Require and pay for teachers to take course work or professional development seminars in the most important documents of American history and government.
2. Provide teacher education to match any new civic education requirements.
3. Review university course requirements and state certification standards for the US history and civics to ensure that teachers are being receiving a proper content education.

Conclusion

We close with bad news and good news about civic education in America. The bad news is that the current state of civic education is poor—in fact, alarming. With other subjects pushing civic education out of the curriculum, very little civics is taught in the elementary and middle school years, and the typical one-semester course in high school is too little, too late. The same is true of US history. Test scores confirm that students are not even "proficient" in their understanding of US history, government, and civics. We are graduating class after class of students who are ill-prepared to take up the responsibilities of citizenship, much less able to provide future leadership in a republic they barely understand and too often fail to appreciate.

But here is the good news: we do not have to sit back and wait for a miracle cure. We do not need to wait for the gridlocked federal government to impose some kind of one-size fits all fix—in fact, we don't even want that. We will not need to depend on some billionaire to rescue civic education by investing tons of money in it (depending on the billionaire's ideas, we may not want that either). This is not a problem so big and complex that any kind of major fix seems beyond us.

Rather, improving civic education depends on many small and medium steps by a wide variety of people, not a big fix by a few. It requires more "all hands on deck" doing what they can, rather than awaiting a savior with a deep pocket and lots of power. In that sense, despite some of the political conflicts that seem to afflict everything these days, including education, there seem to be multiple paths toward real and meaningful progress.

As Ronald Reagan said, it begins with parents at home— reading great books about the American story and its characters, taking their kids to visit historic sites, and talking about national holidays and their purpose. Nothing could put civic education on better footing than parents showing their children that history and civics are important and valuable in the family. Community civic associations of all kinds can reinforce that message.

Then in schools, beginning in kindergarten, we start to build the layer cake of civic knowledge and interest. States should develop goals and standards for introducing age-appropriate subjects and materials in elementary school right on through middle school or junior high school. Classes in other subjects such as reading and spelling, for example, should be encouraged to include some great literature and ideas from US history and the wide world of civic education. This both builds a learning base and develops an interest and even love for citizenship. Robust teacher education and development will be essential to offering these new subjects and materials. At least at the beginning of the reform movement, the NAEP test should be offered in the fourth and eighth grades with results broken down and made available to states, districts, and schools to track how their students are doing.

In high school, every state should have a one-semester course in civic education at a bare minimum, but a full-year course in civics along three years of US history—including the American Founding—should be the goal. The key questions in high school, based on the work that has already been done in earlier grades, should be the "why" questions. The use of primary documents in teaching in high school should be emphasized. Once again, the NAEP test should be required in twelfth grade; other tests, including perhaps the citizenship test, could supplement that.

If we can do those things, we will be well on our way to improved civic education and, more than that, better prepared citizens—even informed patriots. It is worth doing for its own sake, but such a movement will also improve our republic with greater engagement, trust, and understanding for the challenges we face. As James Madison rightly said, "A people who would be their own Governors must arm themselves with the power that knowledge brings."[212] More and better civic education will not fix all our nation's problems, but it has the possibility to greatly improve this experiment in self-government that we love and wish to see sustained.

---

[212] James Madison to W. T. Barry, August 4, 1822, https://tile.loc.gov/storage-services/service/mss/mjm/20//20_0155_0159.pdf.